CHARLOTTE BRONTË
STYLE IN THE NOVEL

THE UNIVERSITY OF WISCONSIN PRESS

CHARLOTTE BRONTË

STYLE IN THE NOVEL

Margot Peters

823.8

Published 1973
The University of Wisconsin Press
Box 1379, Madison, Wisconsin 53701

The University of Wisconsin Press, Ltd.
70 Great Russell Street, London

First printing

Printed in the United States of America

For LC CIP information see the colophon

ISBN 0-299-06240-6

I had great pleasure in reading a few books . . .
preferring always those on whose style or sentiment the writer's individual nature was plainly
stamped; flagging inevitably over characterless
books, however clever and meritorious.

LUCY SNOW: *Villette*

c. 1

CONTENTS

Textual Note

Following is a list of texts used in this study and their abbreviations. Although generally considered the standard text, the Shakespeare Head Brontë edited by T. J. Wise and J. A. Symington, 19 vols. (Oxford, 1931–1938), is in some ways unsatisfactory for the novels. A definitive edition of the Brontë novels is in preparation; the first volume of the Clarendon Edition edited by Ian and Jane Jack has appeared: *Jane Eyre*, edited by Jane Jack and Margaret Smith (Oxford, 1969). For this study I have used the following texts of Brontë's novels, which are readily available to most readers:

P: *The Professor.* London: J. M. Dent & Sons, 1965.
JE: *Jane Eyre.* Edited by Mark Schorer. Boston: Houghton
      Mifflin (Riverside Editions), 1959.
S: *Shirley.* London: J. M. Dent & Sons, 1965.
V: *Villette.* Edited by Geoffrey Tillotson and Donald Hawes.
      Boston: Houghton Mifflin (Riverside Editions), 1971.

CHARLOTTE BRONTË

STYLE IN THE NOVEL

INTRODUCTION

I have attempted this study of Charlotte Brontë's prose style for several reasons. Perhaps the most obvious is that, with the exception of relatively brief discussions of the imagery and symbolism in *Jane Eyre* and *Villette*, no extensive investigation of her style has been made.[1] A further rationale for such a study is to be found in the crucial role played by style and language

1. Some of these essays are: Donald Ericksen, "Imagery as Structure in *Jane Eyre*," *VN* 30 (Fall 1966): 18–22; David Lodge, "Fire and Eyre: The War of the Elements in *Jane Eyre*," *The Language of Fiction* (London, 1966); Eric Solomon, "*Jane Eyre*: Fire and Water," *CE* 25 (December 1963): 215–217; Robert B. Heilman, "Charlotte Brontë, Reason, and the Moon," *NCF* 14 (March 1960): 283–302, and Charlotte Brontë's New Gothic," in *From Jane Austen to Joseph Conrad*, ed. Robert C. Rathburn and Martin Steinmann, Jr. (Minneapolis, 1958), pp. 118–132; Janay Downing, "Fire and Ice Imagery in *Jane Eyre*," *Paunch* 26 (October 1966): 68–78. Karl Kroeber's *Styles in Fictional Structure* (Princeton, 1971), is the most comprehensive treatment of the formal qualities of Brontë's fiction to appear, although it deals less with prose style than with characterization, setting, time, and action. My study, undertaken originally as a thesis under Professor Kroeber, was substantially finished before *Styles in Fictional Structure* appeared.

in the realm of fiction: it is simultaneously the medium with which the novelist creates reality and the vehicle which conveys an attitude toward that reality. Then too, the nature of Charlotte Brontë's prose invites analysis, for while there is no longer any doubt that the study of prose style can yield significant riches, the intensely personal, emotive, idiosyncratic quality of her prose, obvious to even the casual reader, invites the kind of close analysis accorded until relatively recently only to poetry. Finally, efforts to reconcile the precision and objectivity of linguistic analysis with the more intuitive and interpretive discipline of literary criticism seems to me exciting and valuable, and this reconciliation can best take place in the area where both disciplines meet: in stylistics, the scientific study of style.[2]

2. The following bibliographies are excellent guides to the area of stylistics: Richard Bailey and Dolores Burton, *English Stylistics: A Bibliography* (Cambridge, Mass., 1968); Josephine Miles, "Works on Style," *Style and Proportion* (Boston, 1967); Louis T. Milic, *Style and Stylistics* (New York, 1967). Two recent collections of essays in applied linguistics are Donald C. Freeman, ed., *Linguistics and Literary Style* (New York, 1970), and Mark Lester, ed., *Readings in Applied Transformational Grammar* (New York, 1970).

Of the many works on language, linguistics, and stylistics consulted, I would like to mention those which seem to me particularly valuable for their application to literature: the two essays, "On Defining Style: An Essay in Applied Linguistics" by Nils Erik Enkvist, and "An Approach to the Study of Style" by John Spencer and Michael J. Gregory, combined in the volume *Linguistics and Style*, ed. Spencer (London, 1964); Zelig Harris's "Discourse Analysis," *Language* 28 (1952): 1–30; Samuel Levin's *Linguistic Structures in Poetry* (The Hague, 1962), which adapts and expands Harris's principle of "discourse analysis" and is applicable to prose, it seems to me, as well as to poetry; of Roman Jacobson's many writings, his "Closing Statement: Linguistics and Poetics," in *Style in Language*, ed. Thomas A. Sebeok (Cambridge, Mass., 1960), pp. 350–377, and "The Metamorphic and Metonymic Poles," in his and Morris Halle's *Fundamentals of Language* ('s-Gravenhage, 1956), pp. 76–82; Jan Mukarovsky's "Standard Language and Poetic Language," in *Linguistics and Literary Style*, ed. Donald C. Freeman (New York, 1970), pp. 40–56, originally in *A Prague School Reader on Esthetics, Literary Structure, and Style*, ed. and trans. by Paul L. Garvin (Washington, D.C., 1964), pp. 17–30; Stephen Ullmann's *Style in the French Novel* (Cam-

The study of style is characterized at the moment by a diversity of approaches at once challenging and bewildering. There are the more traditional approaches to style practiced by most literary critics. Among the more common is the study of tropes: metaphor, metonymy, synecdoche, analogy. Closely related to this approach to style is the inventory of a writer's lexicon, his use of nonfigurative language. Most frequently, perhaps, traditional style study investigates the imagery of a poem or a novel or of a writer's whole canon: clusters of images drawn from war, finance, religion, or nature are first isolated and then analyzed for what they contribute to the understanding of the work of art and the mind of its creator. When stylistic units other than the word or image are studied, traditional approaches (such as W. K. Wimsatt's *The Prose Style of Samuel Johnson* [1941] or G. Williamson's *The Senecan Amble* [1951]) concentrate chiefly upon such rhetorical devices as parallelism, antithesis, parataxis, and balance. The new criticism, considering elements larger than the sentence as formal or stylistic, has examined the patterns that unify a literary work—the author's "tone," for instance, or point of view, chronological ordering, framing devices, or the structuring effect of recurring patterns of symbolism. When one inventories recent criticism of Conrad's novels or Emily Brontë's *Wuthering Heights*, for example, one finds that the approach has a strong formal bent, concerning itself frequently with such devices as the double narrator point of view or framing techniques. Content has not necessarily been neglected, but it has been approached in the last decades primarily through form.

---

bridge, Eng., 1957), and *Language and Style* (Oxford, 1964); Leo Spitzer's classic *Linguistics and Literary History* (New York, 1962); Richard Ohmann's challenging discussions of the application of generative grammar to the study of style in two essays "Generative Grammars and the Concept of Literary Style," *Word* 20 (December 1964): 423–439, and "Literature as Sentences," *CE* 27 (January 1966): 261–267 (both these essays appear in *Readings in Applied Transformational Grammar,* ed. Lester); also of value is Vernon Lee's *The Handling of Words and Other Studies in Literary Psychology* (New York, 1923), for its perceptive analyses of prose samples from a wide range of writers.

Those linguists—and they are few—who are concerned with the study of style often object, however, that the stylistic criticism of literary scholars deals with matters of content rather than form. They would argue, for example, that an investigation of a writer's lexicon, even though conducted "scientifically," surely involves what is being said rather than how it is being said, and thus belongs outside the realm of stylistics. Most linguists would undoubtedly agree with Richard Ohmann that the methods practiced by most critics of style are interesting in inverse proportion to their emphasis on what we sense as style.[3] That is, the real factors that define a style are not images, tropes, or antithesis considered at random, but the occurrence and distribution of the transformational operations a writer performs upon basic or "kernel" sentences resulting in a characteristic use of relative clauses, deletions, or comparative or negative constructions throughout a text or texts.

Since the mere occurrence of items can tell us something about a writer's style, it is not surprising that style study has turned to the computer and that many recent stylistic analyses have as their starting point long lists of "item" distribution and percentage.[4] Too often, however, these studies end with the lists: missing is an underlying linguistic theory which would systematically and meaningfully relate the data to the notion of

3. Ohmann, "Generative Grammars," in *Readings in Applied Transformational Grammar,* ed. Lester, p. 120. Ohmann believes that none of the present techniques for style analysis has yielded a full and convincing explication of the notion of style, and that critics are working blindly without a theory. Since to Ohmann style is *choice* among different ways of saying the same thing, he proposes that generative grammar with its theory of kernel sentences and *optional* transformations can best provide a coherent theory of the workings of style. To date, Ohmann's suggestion remains a suggestion, albeit a very interesting one.

4. Some recent studies using or evaluating the computer approach to literature are: Edmund A. Bowles, ed., *Computers in Humanistic Research* (Englewood Cliffs, N.J., 1967); John B. Carroll, "Vectors of Prose Style," in *Style in Language,* ed. Sebeok; Louis T. Milic, "The Computer Approach to Style," in *The Art of Victorian Prose,* ed. George Levine and William Madden (London, 1968), pp. 338–361, and *A Quantitative Approach to the Style of Jonathan Swift* (The Hague, 1967).

style. Frequently missing also is the extensive, sensitive, and subjective interpretation of statistical data so essential to any meaningful interpretation of style in its relationship to literature. Thus, despite Ohmann's highly interesting suggestion that transformational generative grammar holds the key to consistent style analysis, the student of style is forced to agree with Karl Uitti's summation of current stylistics in his *Linguistics and Literary Theory* that "no general linguistic theory in America has been implemented in such a way as to deal systematically with the language of literature." It needs to be stressed, of course, that this state of affairs is not discouraging, but challenging.

In this discussion of Charlotte Brontë's prose style I have tried to make the best of two worlds, hoping to avoid the rather daunting lists of computer data and at the same time utilizing the kind of objective, nonpolemical methodology that has been linguistics' most valuable contribution to literary study. Not having the linguist's horror of staining pure form with content, I include a discussion of Charlotte Brontë's language: content and form cannot be expediently divided, and an inclusive study of a writer's style must consider his lexicon. On the other hand, as Ohmann's *Shaw: The Style and the Man* (1962) proves, prose analysis can no longer concern itself with impressionistic reactions to imagery or cadence or trope, but must take into consideration from some systematic, objective approach the morphological, syntactical—and especially in the case of poetry —the phonological levels of language. Hence a chapter on the occurrence, distribution, and effect in Brontë's prose of the adverb—seemingly, perhaps, an inconsequential element of a writer's style.

Since I have not used computerized quantitative analysis to probe Brontë's prose, I have had to rely on some knowledge of nineteenth-century English fiction, a familiarity with Brontë's novels, a background of linguistic study, and a great deal of counting and comparing. The available computerized data on style is, of course, often provocative and useful, although it frequently confirms observation rather than initiates discovery. John B. Carroll's computation of "vectors" that create "personal effect" in style, for example, substantiates what one observes on reading Brontë: that her gripping, personal style is created in part by high numbers of personal pronouns (a necessary corollary of first-person narrative), short words, and active verbs.[5] That the personal rather than the computerized approach to style may still have some value, however, was happily confirmed for me when Professor Karl Kroeber admitted in conversation that although his data revealed that Jane Austen's prose contains more adverbs than Brontë's (see *Styles in Fictional Structure*, "Tabulation Appendices"), Brontë's use of adverbs is indeed more striking and "characteristic" when one takes into account their quality and their syntactical positioning.

Unintentionally, my method resembles perhaps most closely Leo Spitzer's intuitively initiated "philological circle," although "intuition," it would seem, is not the accurate term for that brilliant philologist's recognition of a significant idiosyncracy among the many facets of a writer's prose. That is, rather than beginning with a predetermined list of stylistic items and testing the prose for their occurrence, I began by reading the prose and then investigating further those features which struck me as being the "carriers" of Brontë's highly distinctive voice. After tracing these carriers page by page throughout the four novels, I then chose random samples of prose paragraphs for closer scrutiny and for comparison with passages from other nineteenth-century English novels. Most of the features of Brontë's prose turned out to be highly idiosyncratic: her conspicuous use of inverted syntax, for example, distinguishes Brontë's prose not only from Austen's, but from the prose of Eliot, Dickens, and Thackeray as well.

Michael Riffaterre and the post-Prague school in general have argued that each novel should constitute its own norm

---

5. Carroll, "Vectors of Prose Style." Carroll attempts to identify various objective and subjective dimensions of style which might be used to differentiate both between recognized styles of writing and between great literature and the not-so-great. Carroll admits that he is skeptical whether his statistical study of 150 prose passages of approximately 300 words each accomplished this (p. 284). However, the resulting "prose profiles" of his study seem to me interesting and worthwhile.

and that the deviations from that norm must constitute the style of that text. Applying this theory, an investigator would discover Brontë's use of syntactic inversion: he would find the linguistic pattern of the text broken by "an element which was unpredictable" and which therefore constitutes an element of style.[6] He would not, however, detect the peculiar way Brontë uses adverbs, for this use is the norm throughout her prose rather than the deviation, and is discoverable only by comparison with other texts. Yet the adverb is a noteworthy feature of Brontë's style, and ultimately the significance of a deviation like inversion cannot be estimated without going outside the immediate text for comparison. Doing so, we find that Brontë employs inversion far more than any other nineteenth-century writer of prose fiction, a fact that not only suggests a great deal about the novels themselves, but, more important, helps to evaluate the aesthetic place of her novels in nineteenth-century fiction.

Style, therefore, is not best considered, I believe, as deviation within a textual norm, but more broadly, as choice within an existing code of language. As a human being has an existence both as a private individual and as a type in the history of society, so an author's style is both idiolect and social code—a two-fold phenomenon. Buffon's dictum, "Le style, c'est l'homme même," is thus only half true, for while a writer can choose within the code, the code itself is all that is available to him. We cannot finally evaluate a style unless we assess the possibilities from which an author's choice is made.

Because style is both personal and social, both "ego and world," it may legitimately be explored for significance outside the context of the text itself. Beyond description are the implications of that which has been described. There are few linguists or literary critics who would not agree that the goal of stylistics should be to illumine further the aesthetic, sociological, psychological, or biographical aspects of literature. The philological circle of Leo Spitzer has been criticized for its heavy psy-

6. Michael Riffaterre, "Criteria for Style Analysis," *Word* 15 (April 1959): 154–174.

chological bias and its "formulation of those grand schematic theories about cultural change and history so dear to the German scholarly mind."[7] Spitzer's method is vulnerable to criticism (as what method is not) chiefly because of the temptation for the critic to use known biographical facts to initiate stylistic discoveries in the text. Stephen Ullmann, however, has pointed out (correctly, I believe) that this danger does not essentially affect the value of the method: "As long as the demonstration is conclusive, it surely does not matter in what order the various steps were taken; the main point is that a link has been established between a stylistic peculiarity, its root in the author's psyche, and other manifestations of the same mental factor."[8] The circularity of Spitzer's method is valuable in that after entering the world of the novel, it moves out again to make the vital connection between the mock reality of the novel and the real world—returning the object, as one critic has phrased it, to the continuum of actuality.

To the extent that this investigation of Charlotte Brontë's style utilizes an "in and out" approach it owes a debt to Spitzer and to continental stylistics in general, and to those American style studies of Ohmann, Louis T. Milic, Harold C. Martin, and Norman Holland, for example, which attempt to relate style to personality and era. Insofar as it examines various traits of style in the context of all four Brontë novels, the following study is close in spirit to Ullmann's philosophy, which recognizes the value of examining a stylistic device on the level of the entire work of art. Ullmann's method, however, like much stylistic analysis, remains largely descriptive: having identified and enumerated characteristic prose features, he makes only slender connections between the feature and its impact on the novel as a whole. I have attempted, on the other hand, to integrate prose style and total work of art; not only, in René Wellek and

7. Lodge, *Language of Fiction*, p. 54. For other evaluations of Spitzer, see Bennison Gray, "The Lesson of Leo Spitzer," *MLR* 61 (October 1966): 547–555, and René Wellek, "Leo Spitzer (1887–1960)," *Comparative Literature* 12 (Fall 1960): 310–334.

8. Ullmann, *Style in the French Novel*, pp. 28–29. Besides the excellent descriptive studies of style factors in particular novels, Ullmann's book contains useful stylistic bibliographical material in the footnotes.

Austin Warren's words, to "establish some unifying principle, some general aesthetic aim pervasive of the whole work," but to establish some connection between the reality of the fictional world conveyed through Charlotte Brontë's prose style and the attitude toward this reality communicated simultaneously through the same medium.[9]

It has become fashionable since F. R. Leavis and the new criticism to maintain that there is only one Brontë: the greater part of scholarly writing about the Brontës has been dedicated to Emily and her single novel *Wuthering Heights*. This phenomenon is readily understandable; Charlotte Brontë's novels since their publication have been considered formless—emotional effusions poured forth artlessly under compulsion. Formalistic criticism turned, therefore, to *Wuthering Heights* and its structural problems of chronological ordering, double narrative, and bipartite construction; it eulogized Emily's novel for its structural subtleties and demoted Charlotte's fiction on this basis to a lower rank of achievement.[10] This judgment, I confess, has always seemed unjust to me, both before and after under-

---

9. René Wellek and Austin Warren, *Theory of Literature* (New York, 1956); see particularly the chapter "Style." Christopher Caudwell has stated this dual role of language: "We see, then, that language communicates not simply a dead image of outer reality but also and simultaneously an attitude towards it . . ." (*Illusion and Reality* [New York, 1947], p. 157).

10. Arnold Kettle's essay, "Emily Brontë: *Wuthering Heights*," in his *An Introduction to the English Novel*, 2 vols. (New York, 1960), 1: 5, is one of the few attempts to link *Wuthering Heights* to the Victorian era: "*Wuthering Heights*," says Kettle, "is about England in 1847." Some formal studies of Emily Brontë's novel are: Allen R. Brick, "*Wuthering Heights*: Narrators, Audience, and Message," *CE* 21 (November 1959): 80–86; Vincent Buckley, "Passion and Control in *Wuthering Heights*," *Southern Review* 1 (1964): 5–23; Boris Ford, "*Wuthering Heights*," *Scrutiny* 7 (March 1939): 375–389; C. P. Sanger's well-known essay, "The Structure of *Wuthering Heights*," *Hogarth Essays*, no. 19 (London, 1926), reprinted in *The Brontës*, ed. Ian Gregor (Englewood Cliffs, N.J., 1970), pp. 7–18; Mark Schorer, "Fiction and the 'Matrix of Analogy,'" *Kenyon Review* 11 (Autumn 1949): 539–560; Melvin Watson, "Tempest in the Soul: The Theme and Structure of *Wuthering Heights*," *NCF* 4 (September 1949): 87–100; Carl Woodring, "The Narrators of *Wuthering Heights*," *NCF* 11 (March 1957): 298–305.

taking to become more thoroughly acquainted with Charlotte Brontë's four novels. First, form alone does not make excellence. Second, the structure of *Wuthering Heights* is its weakest point. Only the force of Emily Brontë's prose and the strange power of her story overcome the egregious structural mistake she commits in killing off her heroine halfway through the novel and ending one of the most famous love affairs in fiction at mid-point. Emily Brontë's second book probably would have avoided this error of inexperience.

Recent critical writing about Charlotte Brontë's novels— also predictably—has attempted to rescue her fiction from the limbo of formlessness by claiming a conscious and developing artistry in her four mature novels, *The Professor, Jane Eyre, Shirley,* and *Villette.* Much of this criticism is fruitful: few readers will deny, I believe, that *Jane Eyre* is the coherent and economically structured novel that W. A. Craik, Earl Allen Knies, and Melvin Watson, for example, argue it to be.[11] Attempts to find structural strengths in *Shirley* are less convincing: it must be judged a formally unsuccessful novel, a broad scheme poorly executed, latently rich and powerful, but remarkable chiefly for the vitality of characters like Shirley, the Yorkes, and the ubiquitous curates.[12] Most important, perhaps, has been the critical attention focused upon Charlotte Brontë's last novel, *Villette,* a book until lately obscured by the glamorous and enduring appeal of *Jane Eyre.* Recent criticism by Robert Colby, Inga-Stina Ewbank, E. D. H. Johnson, and W. A. Craik has undertaken to show that the more diffuse and complex form of *Villette* is highly purposeful in that it records, to use Colby's phrase, the life of the mind of its heroine, Lucy Snowe, and that Brontë's last book is therefore a more subtle

11. W. A. Craik, *The Brontë Novels* (London, 1968), see especially p. 85; Earl Allen Knies, *The Art of Charlotte Brontë* (Athens, Ohio, 1969); Melvin Watson, "Form and Substance in the Brontë Novels," in *From Jane Austen to Joseph Conrad,* ed. Rathburn and Steinmann, pp. 106–117.

12. See, for example, Ivy Holgate, "The Structure of *Shirley,*" *Brontë Society Transactions* 14 (1962): 27–35; Jacob Korg, "The Problem of Unity in *Shirley,*" *NCF* 12 (September 1957): 125–136. Watson argues in "Form and Substance in the Brontë Novels" that, potentially, *Shirley* is a better novel than *Jane Eyre.*

and artistically mature work than the straightforward *Jane Eyre*.[13] Studies in the imagery and symbolism of Charlotte Brontë's novels, the best of which is perhaps David Lodge's chapter on *Jane Eyre* in *The Language of Fiction*, have also sought to emphasize the formal coherence discoverable in such deliberate and recurring patterns.[14] The most valuable assessment of the formal characteristics of Charlotte Brontë's novels to appear is Kroeber's recent *Styles in Fictional Structure*, which gives a perceptive, comparative interpretation of statistically gathered data on the novels of Austen, Brontë, and George Eliot, and at the same time significantly expands the notion of style to include formal aspects of setting, character, time, and action.

Less attention, it seems to me, has been devoted to exploring the content of Charlotte Brontë's works, although investigations of how a writer says things must necessarily involve discussing what is said. Robert Martin and Ewbank's book-length studies of the novels, Robert Colby's remarks on *Villette* in *Fiction with a Purpose*, and Kathleen Tillotson's intelligent discussion of *Jane Eyre* in *Novels of the Eighteen-Forties* are exceptions in their attempt to relate Brontë's fiction to a sociological, cultural, or psychological context.[15]

13. Robert Colby, "*Villette* and the Life of the Mind," *PMLA* 75 (1960): 410–419; Inga-Stina Ewbank, *Their Proper Sphere* (London, 1966); E. D. H. Johnson, "Daring the Dread Glance: Charlotte Brontë's Treatment of the Supernatural in *Villette*," *NCF* 20 (March 1966): 325–336; Craik, *The Brontë Novels*.

14. See my footnote 1 above and also Charles Burkhart, "Another Key Word for *Jane Eyre*," *NCF* 16 (September 1961): 177–179, and "Brontë's *Villette*," *Explicator* 21 no. 1, item 8 (September 1962); Richard Chase, "The Brontës: A Centennial Observance," *Kenyon Review* 9 (Autumn 1947): 487–506; Herbert R. Coursen, "Storm and Calm in *Villette*," *Discourse* 5 (Winter 1961–1962): 318–333.

15. Robert Martin, *The Accents of Persuasion: Charlotte Brontë's Novels* (London, 1966); Ewbank, *Their Proper Sphere;* Kathleen Tillotson, *Novels of the Eighteen-Forties* (Oxford, 1954); Robert Colby's concern in *Fiction with a Purpose* (Bloomington, Ind., 1967), is "the relationship of authors to their original literary environment . . . and the novels themselves as repositories of literary history" (p. 6); he argues that *Jane Eyre* and *Villette* contain much that was current.

To establish such a relationship is the ultimate goal of this study of Charlotte Brontë's style. Admittedly it may seem perverse to approach this objective through the formal medium of style. Undeniably, an objective description of Brontë's prose occupies the bulk of this discussion. Yet I hope that a further understanding of the vitality of Charlotte Brontë's conflict with Victorian culture and the fiction it produced will emerge from these pages, for this conflict is what establishes Charlotte as the more important Brontë.

But this is to anticipate.

1

THE EMPHATIC ADVERB

The suggestion was sensible; and yet I could not force myself to act on it. I so dreaded a reply that would crush me with despair. To prolong doubt was to prolong hope. I might yet once more see the Hall under the ray of her star. There was the stile before me—the very fields through which I had hurried, blind, deaf, distracted, with a revengeful fury tracking and scourging me, on the morning I fled from Thornfield: ere I well knew what course I had resolved to take, I was in the midst of them. How fast I walked! How I ran sometimes! How I looked forward to catch the first view of the well-known woods! With what feelings I welcomed single trees I knew, and familiar glimpses of meadow and hill between them!

At last the woods rose; the rookery clustered dark; a loud cawing broke the morning stillness. Strange delight inspired me: on I hastened. Another field crossed—a lane threaded—and there were the courtyard walls—the back offices: the house itself, the rookery still hid. "My first view of it shall be in front," I determined, "where its bold battlements will strike the eye nobly at once, and where I can single out my master's very window: perhaps he will be standing at it—he rises early: perhaps he is now walking in the orchard, or on the pavement in front. Could I but see him!—but a moment! Surely, in that

case, I should not be so mad as to run to him? I cannot tell—
I am not certain." (*JE*, p. 402)

A knowledgeable reader, coming across this passage out of
context, would be almost certain to recognize the impassioned
accents appealing to him from the page. The signature of
Charlotte Brontë's style is stamped upon every sentence, every
phrase, almost upon every word. If, as one Victorian man of
letters claimed, the greatness of the writer can be measured by
the individuality of his style, then Charlotte Brontë must be a
great writer indeed.[1] Early Victorian taste, which preferred the
strongly personal element in prose, did not prevail, however;
and Charlotte Brontë's writing, like that of other highly idiosyncratic authors, has been as strongly condemned as it has
been highly praised. But while critics have been free with impressionistic labels like "overwrought and uneven," or "powerful and poetic," no sustained attempt has been made to subject
impression to stylistic analysis, an effort this study proposes to
undertake.

Given a prose bristling with almost as many stylistic eccen-
tricities as Carlyle's, it is perhaps necessary to explain why a
discussion of Charlotte Brontë's style should begin with the
adverb.[2] The reasons are several. Very like a small pupil snap-
ping his fingers for attention, this small unit of expression seems
to clamor loudest for notice when the novels are read with attention to style, and thus to demand silencing at once. And
then, after even a cursory appraisal, it appears that larger
questions of syntax might best be approached by ascertaining
first what Charlotte Brontë does syntactically with single parts

---

1. Travis R. Merritt, "Taste, Opinion, and Theory in the Rise of
Victorian Prose Stylism," in *The Art of Victorian Prose*, ed. George
Levine and William Madden (London, 1968), pp. 3–38; p. 19, quoting
T. H. Wright's "Style," *Macmillan's* (November 1877).

2. Linguistic terminology is so complex that to call the part of speech
discussed in this chapter an adverb is to oversimplify. Yet I have chosen
this word rather than attempting at all points to distinguish between
adverbs (morphologically defined), adverbials (positionally defined),
qualifiers (closed word list), etc. The adverb class as a whole cannot be
defined without great complications.

of speech, since this minor stylistic trait seems to foreshadow a major aspect of her style. Behind both these reasons, however, lies a deeper question of linguistic theory. Traditionally, keys to an author's style have been sought in his diction, in his rhetorical devices, or in his imagery. But modern linguistics has shown that the most telling characteristics of style are often to be discovered outside the lexical area of language in the ways an author handles word order, or verb tense, or conjunctions, or even in the way he omits or adds the article before nouns.[3] Recognizing the importance of the syntactical and morphological "layers" of language in assessing style by no means invalidates studies of imagery or rhetoric, but it does provide a rationale for beginning with what perhaps seems a minor stylistic trait.

One of the most striking characteristics of Charlotte Brontë's use of the adverb is the frequency with which it occurs. Only a count of every adverb in every line of every Victorian novel would give a definitive description of the presence of this form class, but such exactitude is neither feasible nor necessary: this study must trust to limited samples of prose to make its point, passages of 500 words chosen at random from the four Brontë novels, and, for the sake of comparison, from other works of eighteenth- and nineteenth-century prose fiction. In the paragraphs from *Jane Eyre* at the beginning of this chapter, for example, we find 32 adverbs in 267 words, 52 in the entire 500-word passage.[4] Even without dashing to the bookcase to

3. The view, for example, of Stephen Ullmann, *Style in the French Novel* (Cambridge, Eng., 1957), p. 17; and Louis T. Milic, "The Computer Approach to Style," in *The Art of Victorian Prose*, ed. Levine and Madden, pp. 338–361.

4. This number does not include adverbial prepositional phrases, adverbials introducing subordinate adverbial clauses, infinitive phrase adverbials, participial phrase adverbials. I have included noun-phrase adverbials: "I left *Sunday morning*." For the problem of verb-adverbial composites, I have followed generally the principles offered in Norman C. Stageberg's *An Introductory English Grammar*, 2d ed. (New York: Holt, Rinehart and Winston, 1965, repr. 1971), p. 224: meaning, immovability, inseparability.

make comparisons, a reader must feel that the adverb content—
approximately one adverb for every ten words—is unusually
high.

Further assessment of passages chosen at random from the
novels (avoiding dialogue) bears out the first impression.
Taking the novels chronologically, sixteen 500-word samples
show the following adverb count: *The Professor*: 38 (pp. 47–
48: "Next morning . . . in French"), 46 (pp. 103–104: "If I . . .
his business"), 37 (pp. 163–164: "When Pelet . . . old suitor"),
39 (pp. 217–218: "In two months . . . bright"); *Jane Eyre*: 45
(pp. 107–108: "This lane . . . exactly"), 37 (pp. 347–348: "I continued . . . exciting"), 49 (pp. 297–298: "When once . . . nature"),
52 (pp. 402–403: "The suggestion . . . asleep"); *Shirley*: 41
(pp. 231–232: "But this . . . slender"), 35 (pp. 372–373: "With
any . . . of his"), 29 (pp. 442–443: "Briarmains . . . hand"), 43
(pp. 482–483: "I said . . . storm"); *Villette*: 46 (pp. 11–12:
"Some days . . . out mad"), 42 (pp. 137–138: "I err . . . sorrow
in"), 34 (pp. 349–350: "I lent . . . to all"), 35 (pp. 295–296:
"Yet . . . upon him"). The average is 40.5 adverbs per passage.

At this point it becomes necessary to confirm impression
by comparison. Five-hundred-word passages from novels by
Defoe, Austen, Dickens, Eliot, Scott, and Thackeray contain the
following number of adverbs per sample: *Moll Flanders*: 35, 25;
Emma: 25, 33, 38; *David Copperfield*: 22, 27; *Great Expectations*: 22, 28; *Middlemarch*: 32, 17, 24; *The Mill on the Floss*:
25; *Adam Bede*: 23, 30, 43; *Old Mortality*: 29, 13; *Henry
Esmond*: 29, 35, 24; *Vanity Fair*: 21, 24, 36.[5] Allowing for the

5. Daniel Defoe, *Moll Flanders* (New York, 1950): pp. 121–122 ("If
this . . . I"), pp. 163–164 (But it . . . women"); Jane Austen, *Emma*
(Middlesex, Eng., 1966): pp. 51–52 ("Mr. Woodhouse . . . thought herself"), pp. 56–57 ("Harriet Smith's . . . talkativeness"), pp. 217–218
("There was . . . up her"); Charles Dickens, *David Copperfield* (Boston,
1958): pp. 208–209 ("Why do . . . resolve"), pp. 316–317 ("Until the
. . . one of"); Dickens, *Great Expectations* (Middlesex, Eng., 1965):
pp. 212–213 ("I found . . . reading and"), pp. 352–353 ("The influences
. . . horrors"); George Eliot, *Middlemarch* (Middlesex, Eng., 1965):
pp. 212–213 ("Dr. Minchin . . . take it"), pp. 229–230 ("On other . . .
She had"), pp. 456–457 ("This sore . . . good deal"); Eliot, *The Mill on
the Floss* (New York, 1962): pp. 179–180 ("The alternations . . . softness
of"); Eliot, *Adam Bede* (New York, 1963): pp. 202–204 ("But Adam

chance that immediately following the 29-adverb passage from *Old Mortality* there lies in wait one containing 43 or even 53, twenty-four samplings must give a fairly accurate indication of the quantity of adverbs used by several other writers. The average of 27.5 is significantly lower than the 40.5 average found in Charlotte Brontë's prose.

Vernon Lee, while using the method, has questioned the relevance of comparative word counts since content must, after all, decide what word classes an author consciously or unconsciously elects to emphasize.[6] Beyond instinctive and prevailing choices of linguistic expression, a deft writer certainly varies his style to some extent to suit situations, so that this objection has some relevance. It is of interest, therefore, to compare word count in several passages, although—admittedly—equating content is impossible. Two scenes come readily to mind because of their similarity to the famous "red-room" chapter of *Jane Eyre*: Maggie Tulliver's self-incarceration in the attic after the stormy interview with Tom over the dead rabbits in *The Mill on the Floss*, and the imprisonment of David Copperfield in his room by the sinister Murdstones. Counting, we find that Eliot, whose prose samples averaged 27.7 adverbs, now uses 52 in 500 words to describe Maggie's dreary afternoon of exile (pp. 43–44: "Maggie stood . . . where's the"), while Dickens, who had averaged 24.7, now employs 42 (pp. 52–53: "He beat . . . my jailor"). Both Eliot and Dickens are thus writing here at an "adverbial pitch" which in Charlotte Brontë's prose seems to be the rule rather than the exception. This would seem to indicate that content has somehow demanded a departure from the ordinary.

. . . for an"), pp. 362–363 ("Our good . . . reader"), pp. 405–406 ("At Stoniton . . . to Adam"); Sir Walter Scott, *Old Mortality* (London, 1964): pp. 78–79 ("Although . . . were"), pp. 250–252 ("But as . . . and"); William Thackeray, *Henry Esmond* (Middlesex, Eng., 1970): pp. 109–110 ("A pretty . . . join him"), pp. 288–289 ("The effect . . . before Her"), pp. 413–415 ("Besides . . . after his"); Thackeray, *Vanity Fair* (New York, 1962): pp. 78–80 ("Sir Pitt . . . She"), pp. 400–401 "Jos's London . . . world like"), pp. 528–529 ("Here . . . when she").

6. Vernon Lee, *The Handling of Words and Other Studies in Literary Psychology* (New York, 1923), p. 195.

However, if an author varied his style extensively, if every new situation called for different sentence rhythms, different imagery, a new phraseology, no author would possess a style at all. It is the writer who shapes reality according to his interpretation of it. Content dictates form, but then, it is the writer who determines the content and casts it in a style that reflects his vision of its significance. Thus Jane Austen almost invariably describes all situations in a lady-like way: it is the primness of her phraseology which gives Louisa Musgrove's tragic fall, for example, the bathetic quality of a marionette's opera, as Sir Herbert Read has so aptly phrased it.[7] And since the Eliot and Dickens passages still sound like Eliot and Dickens, and not Charlotte Brontë, we must conclude that not only the quantity of a word class must be considered— important as that may be—but other characteristics as well.

II

It becomes clear after reading a few pages of Brontë prose that the syntactical position these adverbs occupy signals as loudly for attention as their numbers. While an adverb can be partially defined morphologically as a class of word that takes the suffixes -*ly*, -*wise*, and the free-form *like*, adverbs/adverbials cannot be described syntactically without enormous complication because of their extreme mobility within the sentence. The following examples illustrate only the most common positions this form class can occupy: (1) He would *seldom* make the effort; (2) *Now* she must go; (3) She drove *recklessly*; (4) He *actually* expects a profit; (5) They will play chess *tomorrow*. A skillful writer, given the syntactic flexibility of the adverb, would normally exploit this characteristic to create various effects of emphasis, meaning, or tone.

But conspicuously, in cases which involve stylistic choice, Charlotte Brontë locates the adverb in positions which jar the reader's attention into a more than ordinary awareness of its

7. Herbert Read, *English Prose Style* (New York, 1928), p. 120.

presence. The following sentences taken from the first few chapters of *Villette* illustrate this phenomenon:[8]

> I was *not long* allowed the amusement of this study of character. (p. 25)

> ". . . you should not feel so much pain when you are *very soon* going to rejoin your father." (p. 29)

> Thus tranquillized and cherished she *at last* slumbered. (p. 29)

> However, it cannot be concealed that, in that case, I must *somehow* have fallen over-board . . . . (p. 30)

> ". . . contrasted with the existence you have *lately* led, it may appear tolerable." (p. 30)

> "What if . . . I am *yet* destined to enjoy health?" (p. 33)

> It was terrible to think of *again* encountering those bearded, sneering simpletons . . . . (p. 54)

> I *fixedly* looked at the street-stones . . . . (p. 55)

> . . . though we made *together* an awful clamour . . . we achieved little progress. (p. 55)

> The little man fixed *on me* his spectacles. (p. 56)

> . . . she opened a little memorandum-book, *coolly* perused its contents, and took *from between the leaves* a small plaited lock of Miss Marchmont's grey hair. (p. 59)

In virtually all of these cases (two prepositional phrases have been included to indicate that this trend extends also to them), the sentence would have sounded more natural had the adverb occupied a different slot: "I was not allowed the amusement of this study of character *long*"; or "I looked *fixedly* at the street-stones"; or "The little man fixed his spectacles *on me*." This wrenching of syntax is not an occasional stylistic trick, but a prevailing mode of expression in Charlotte Brontë's

8. I have italicized words in quotations from Brontë's and other authors' writings throughout the text of this work in order to emphasize points of style. Words italicized by Brontë are indicated by small capitals.

novels. Even though three "normal" sentences could be found for every one of the type illustrated above, this idiosyncrasy would be striking. A comparison with several sentences from *Vanity Fair* (pp. 400-401: 24 adverbs) shows the very different method of Thackeray:

> He sent round prospectuses to his friends . . . and talked *pompously* about making his fortune *still.*
>
> "I was better off *once*, sir," he did not fail to tell everybody . . . .
>
> "But the Sedleys were *always* a proud family."
>
> You and I, my dear reader, may drop into this condition *one day* . . . .
>
> . . . and there was only his wife in all the world who fancied . . . that he was *still* doing any business *there.*

All of these sentences sound natural, conversational, and inconspicuous to a native speaker of English. Had Charlotte Brontë written them they would probably have had an entirely different effect: " 'I was *once* better off, sir' "; or "You and I, my dear reader, may *one day* drop into this condition"; or "and *pompously* talked about *still* [she would have used *yet*] making his fortune."

The effect of Brontë's positioning the adverb before the verb, or between the auxiliary and the main verb, or before the direct object is to give particular stress to the adverb while at the same time eclipsing through a relatively reduced stress the verb and its object. In the sentence "I fíxedly looked at the street-stones," the word *fixedly* receives more stress than any other word, whereas if "normal" word order had been observed, the heaviest stress in the sentence would have fallen on *street*: "I looked at the stréet-stones fixedly." Similarly: "we made togéther an awful clamour" / "we made an awful clámour together"; "she opened a little memorandum-book, cóolly perûsed" / "she opened a little memorandum-book, perûsed côolly." Almost any paragraph in any of Charlotte Brontë's novels will reveal the same phenomenon. In the passage from *Jane Eyre* given at the beginning of the chapter, despite the most striking and evocative vocabulary of sentences two and four—*dread, crush, despair, the Hall, ray, star*—it is the adverbs *so* and *yet once more* which steal the show by virtue of their stressed syntactic position.

Taken together, adverbial frequency and stress shed some light on the psychology of the author who uses them so conspicuously. It seems evident that to Charlotte Brontë both the action and its object are eclipsed in importance by the way an act is performed—its duration, its intensity, its manner. The street-stones and the act of looking at them are less important in Charlotte Brontë's view of reality than the manner in which one looks—fixedly. Similarly, the fact that Miss Marchmont slumbered is less significant than the fact that she slumbered *at last*, a phrase which invokes the suffering and endurance of both Miss Marchmont and Lucy Snowe. All else is subordinate to the fact that the little man fixed his spectacles *on me*; and the chief significance of Madame Beck's persual of the little memorandum book is that she examined it *coolly*. The English language, the available code, determines ultimately the ways its speakers can view experience; it provides, in Richard Ohmann's phrase, "the epistemic bias" from which a writer cannot escape, a phenomenon demonstrated perhaps most persuasively by Benjamin Lee Whorf.[9] Within the circumference of epistemological possibility dictated by language is ample room for personal vision, made possible by the existence of choice within the code.

To a writer like Thackeray who views the world sardonically and presents it to us from a bemused and critical distance, who is often as interested in veiling his characters' motives and feelings as he is in revealing them, the expression potential of the adverb is apt to be a matter of relatively little importance. An author whose detachment exhibits "the impossibility of self-knowledge and, in the fullest sense, dramatic change" can scarcely be interested in exploiting a linguistic entity which

9. See Richard Ohmann, "Prolegomena to the Analysis of Prose Style," in *Style in Prose Fiction,* ed. Harold C. Martin (New York, 1959), pp. 1–24; Benjamin Lee Whorf, *Language, Thought, and Reality,* ed. John B. Carroll (New York, 1956).

offers the means of exploring the possibility of self-knowledge.[10] For a writer like Charlotte Brontë, however, whose chief pre-occupation is with self-knowledge and self-expression, the adverb must be—consciously or unconsciously— a crucial element of stylistic expression. For Charlotte Brontë is seldom content with determining merely that her pulse beats: she must note anxiously at what rate, and with what force, and with what fluctuations.

III

Yet to say that Charlotte Brontë uses adverbs frequently and in stressed positions is still not to say enough about this peculiarity of style: the quality of the words must be taken into account. *Here* and *fervently* are both adverbs, yet the two sentences, "He asked me here," and, "He asked me fervently," convey two quite different degrees of semantic intensity. Let us go back at this point to the episode from *The Mill on the Floss* mentioned earlier, Maggie in the attic, a passage containing 52 adverbs, unusually many for George Eliot. Assessing the quality of these words, we find that 14 of the 52 are adverbs of time: *then, now, soon, presently,* etc.; and that 13 are adverbs denoting place: *there, up, home, in, out.* Thus 27—more than half—of the adverbs (not including *never*) are "neutral" verbal modifiers; that is, they are denotative of external and measurable facts about the action taking place.

This is not surprising in a scene which is described objectively from the omniscient author point of view: "These bitter sorrows of childhood! when sorrow is all new and strange, when hope has not yet got wings to fly beyond the days and weeks, and the space from Summer to Summer seems measureless." When, however, George Eliot reports Maggie's point of view, reverting to *style indirect libre* to express a child's experience

10. G. Armour Craig, "On the Style of *Vanity Fair*," in *Style in Prose Fiction*, ed. Martin, pp. 85–113.

in a child's words, adverbs change in quality, tending now to designate degrees of feeling rather than outer phenomena. "She would *never* go down" expresses not something measurably temporal but a child's impression of the infinite duration of hurt pride. Other adverbs used to intensify abstract adjectives communicate the same childish exaggeration: *how* happy, *very* cruel, *how very* sorry, *too* miserable. These, of course, are very close to what one linguist calls "catch-all intensifiers," terms used so often that their charge is extremely weak.[11] They are appropriate here because they are childlike and ingenuous and because they are used by Maggie herself rather than by the tolerant but faintly amused narrator, but their effect is mock-tragic and rather superficial. Of the 52 adverbs, only *never*, used four times, can be said really to intensify Maggie's experience; this is consistent with the way the episode is presented to us, through a veil of sympathetic irony, from a distance. The fact that the adverbs frequently receive no special stress within the sentence supports the conclusion that, despite their frequency in this particular passage, this form class is not of great importance to Eliot as a vehicle of expression: in the following sentence, for example, emphasis falls on *Tom, happy,* and *cruel:* "Tóm was come *home,* and she had thought *how* háppy she would be,—and *now* he was crúel to her."

David Copperfield's beating and imprisonment is so like the red-room chapter of *Jane Eyre,* written two years earlier, that it is certain Dickens used Brontë's novel for inspiration. Both children are dragged away forcibly and locked up; both children are smitten with guilt (a Victorian child's prevailing state of mind) at their behavior ("Was I a criminal?"; "All said I was wicked and perhaps I might be so"); both children catch distorted glimpses of themselves in a mirror, and so forth. And Dickens here is much closer in spirit to Charlotte Brontë than Eliot could ever be. His chief concern, however, is with action and plot, a fact which can be deduced both from the shortness of the imprisonment episode, which involves little more than a

11. Harold C. Martin, "The Development of Style in Nineteenth-Century American Fiction," in *Style in Prose Fiction,* ed. Martin, pp. 114–141.

page, and from the quality of the adverbs, which reflect a dominant concern with placing the action in the temporal and spatial world by means of such words as *then, there, afresh, the while, long after, next morning, every morning, up, out, there, open.* Relatively few adverbs qualify David's behavior: *how well, almost, listlessly, so, fearfully, solemnly.*

Qualitative analysis of the adverbs in all four passages from Dickens cited above reveals the same tendency. In the *David Copperfield* samples many adverbs of place and sequential time occur: *behind, there, forward, then, first, next, now,* and so forth. In *Great Expectations* we find *together, round, up, upright, presently, still, then,* etc. Less frequently occur terms describing the manner of action: *hardly, immoderately, madly,* for example. From this evidence it can be concluded that Dickens is occupied to a great degree with the exterior aspect of action; that he has a strong pictorial sense which leads him to define action in terms of place and a strong sense of plot tempo which manifests itself in adverbs denoting the chronological passage of time.

When we compare the Eliot and Dickens scenes with a 500-word passage chosen at random from chapter 2 of *Jane Eyre* (pp. 14–15: "Superstition . . . in capacity"), differences in adverbial quality already hinted at emerge. Of the 41 adverbs, 12 indicate time and place—approximately one-fourth compared to one-half in Eliot and almost one-half in Dickens. There are no modifiers which come close to being "catch-all intensifiers." Like Dickens, unlike Eliot, many adverbs (not counting *not*) qualify the action, words like *universally, bluntly, thus, wantonly, equally, as little, clearly,* etc. Seven emotionally connotative adverbs of indefinite time occur—*always, forever, never, more*—compared to four in Eliot and one in Dickens, and of these, six receive main stress, indicating their importance.

Different values thus emerge from such an investigation. In Charlotte Brontë we find a person highly concerned with the nuance of behavior, with the drama of feeling rather than of action, so that her temporal adverbs are of a different sort, and function in a different way. In the Eliot passage, many of the adverbs are used to establish a logical sequence of events:

"Maggie *soon* thought she had been hours in the attic"; "she would stay up there and starve herself . . . and *then* they would all be frightened"; "but *presently* she began to cry *again*"; "but *then* the need of being loved"; etc. In Brontë's novels, however, adverbs of time are often really words denoting the timelessness of reality—of suffering, of anxiety—and thus delineate no logical, external ticking by of minutes or of hours, no definite marshalling of events in sequence, but internal (and eternal) states of mind: ". . . my blood was *still* warm; the mood of the revolted slave was *still* bracing me . . . . Why was I *always* suffering, *always* browbeaten, *always* accused, *for ever* condemned? . . . I could not answer the ceaseless inward question —WHY I *thus* suffered; *now*, at the distance of—I will not say *how* many years, I see it clearly."

The juxtaposition of *then* with *now* in the last sentence is a frequent mode of contrast in the novels. Of course, the form of narrative reminiscence invites this contrast of narrator-now with narrator-at-the-time-of-the-event-he-is-recounting, yet other first-person narratives do not play upon this particular temporal theme (one thinks of *Moll Flanders, Pamela, David Copperfield, Great Expectations*). In Brontë's novels, however, this device is conspicuous—not least because of the supralinguistic italicization of *then* or *now*. Usually the contrast involves, not action (I used to run away, but now I stand and fight), but internal processes of thinking, feeling or understanding: "[then] I could not answer the ceaseless inward question . . . now . . . I see it clearly"; or, "I felt myself superior to that check *then* as I do *now*."

This adverbial peculiarity suggests several things, one of which is hit upon by Rochester in his words to Jane: " 'You think all existence lapses in as quiet a flow as that in which your youth has hitherto slid away' " (*JE*, p. 136). Rochester is half-wrong and half-right about this quiet flow. Brontë's protagonists lead lives devoid of much external event with the result that they dwell on, analyze, and exaggerate both the event and their reaction to it. (The process would seem to be circular: they have so little social intercourse that they must live intensely in themselves, and they need so little social contact because they do live so intensely in themselves.) In lives which pass slowly, undisturbed by outward fluctuation—Jane is three months at Thornfield without incident—time is measured in terms of the ebb and flow of states of mind; of mental health or sickness which is often reflected in physical illness so that frequently terms for describing both time passage and illness merge in phrases like "morning wasted," or "the year sickened." The existence of the Brontë protagonist is the opposite of measuring out life in coffee spoons. In retrospect, therefore, it is the contrast or similarity of states of mind that have drama and significance for the Brontë protagonist: *then* I felt that, *now* I feel this. In Charlotte Brontë's own life this same phenomenon can be seen in her letters to Ellen Nussey, to Smith or Williams, to Mrs. Gaskell. Life in the Haworth parsonage is not measured by events (they are few), but by eras of feeling—months of hypochondria, for example, or a spring in which Charlotte is in relatively elastic spirits.[12]

The effect in the novels of this juxtaposition of time planes is to call attention to the "presence" of the narrator as he exists at some point in time outside the action he is narrating. In some cases the device is functional, as in the childhood chapters of *Jane Eyre* where the *then-now* contrast serves to explain to the reader situations which the child Jane could not possibly have interpreted. In other cases, such as Crimsworth's letter to Charles, where the contrast is between the narrator's reaction to past events which he is recalling for his friend (now) and his reactions in a still more distant past as a youth, the device seems gratuitous: we do not really care about the narrator's existence beyond the confines of the immediate story he is telling us. The contrast seems to be dictated not by exigencies of plot, but by an instinctive desire to achieve dramatic contrast with a theme that is always of interest to the author herself.

A time-sense like this is quite different from the time-sense evidenced by Defoe in *Moll Flanders*:

12. For Charlotte Brontë's collected letters, see Clement Shorter, *The Brontës, Life and Letters,* 2 vols. (New York, 1908); and T. J. Wise and J. A. Symington, eds., *The Brontës: Their Lives, Friendships, and Correspondence,* 4 vols. (Oxford, 1932).

He appointed the same evening, after the bank was shut and business over, for me to meet him . . . . After the first meeting . . . we parted, and he appointed me to come the next day . . . when I entered more freely with him into my case. . . . However, we had not much more discourse at that time . . . but that if I would come home to his house after their business was over, he would by that time consider what might be done for me . . . . When I came he made several proposals for my placing my money in the bank . . . ." (pp. 122–124)

Here time is measured out rapidly in terms of business deals and the hours or days it takes to realize them. From Defoe's example, we can deduce that the more preoccupied with the material world an author is, the more he can identify with the goals of the materialistic, bourgeois society of which he is a part, the more conscious he will be of time and its effect upon his life, since, quite literally, time means profit. At the opposite pole from Defoe is a writer like Virginia Woolf, who, as an aesthetician alienated from twentieth-century materialism, casts logical time sequence to the winds, so that, in Eric Auerbach's words, "exterior events have actually lost their hegemony" and serve only to "release and interpret inner events."[13]

Charlotte Brontë stands between these two writers. As the daughter of a poor, Tory clergyman she is at once conservatively wedded to Victorian bourgeois institutions and in rebellion at the limitations with which they circumscribe her life. Lacking the narrative sophistication of the stream-of-consciousness technique and a psychological ability to explore multipersonal areas of consciousness (the term is Auerbach's), she still evidences in her novels a concern with time as it is experienced beyond mere chronological event in the timeless realm of emotional and moral development.

Another stylistic characteristic, directly related to the time-sense discussed above, is Brontë's infrequent use of adverbs which diminish rather than intensify. These are in a minority in all the prose examined, but there are significantly fewer in

13. Eric Auerbach, *Mimesis,* trans. Willard R. Trask (Princeton, 1968), p. 538.

Brontë's prose. George Eliot is prone to diminishing or tentative adverbs: the three passages from *Middlemarch* contain many of this type: *a little, only, quite, not so, less, hardly* are examples. Without taking content into consideration, we can feel behind the prose of *Middlemarch* the careful mind of a person not given to emotional absolutes, a person who weighs experience according to finely graded degrees of relativity. When content is, experimentally, taken into account, we find Eliot using the diminishing adverb to describe the nocturnal bedroom scene in *Adam Bede*, using it skillfully to expose Hetty Sorrel's narcissism and to emphasize her moral and mental limitations by means of terms like *just, only, little, simply, gradually, merely.* We find, however, that whether Charlotte Brontë approves or disapproves of a character, she is generally unable to express her judgment in words which imply an objective and subtle analysis of personality, and that her protagonists seldom experience any emotion that is not emphatic.

This characteristic helps explain the different effect of Jane Austen's style. Since prose samples from *Emma* show a high number of adverbs, and since adverbs have been identified in Brontë with intensity, Charlotte Brontë's claim that Austen ruffles her reader by nothing vehement, disturbs him by nothing profound" might seem unfounded.[14] Many of Austen's adverbs, however, are mitigating—*not so leniently, almost immediately, only, only moderately, could hardly*—modifiers which tend to dilute rather than emphasize, and to give her characters that air of civilized consciousness appropriate to actors in a novel of manners. A further linguistic explanation of the very different effect of Austen's adverbs can be found in their syntactic position: "There was one person among his new acquaintance in Surrey *not so leniently* disposed. In general he was judged, throughout the parishes of Donwell and Highbury, with great candour; liberal allowances were made for the little excesses of such a handsome young man—one who smiled *so often* and bowed *so well* . . ." (*Emma*, p. 217). In the first sen-

---

14. Letter to W. S. Williams, April 12th, 1850, in Wise and Symington, eds., *The Brontës*, 3: 98–99.

tence, heaviest stress falls on *one* and *disposed;* in the second, stress falls on words immediately adjacent to the adverbs, that is, on *smiled* and *bowed,* clearly indicating that Jane Austen does not intend to load adverbs with more than ordinary power.

Similarly, in a passage from *Tom Jones* containing 47 adverbs, it is the quality rather than the quantity of the adverbs which is significant, as the following examples show: "one of the *most* superstitious of men," "for so he *most firmly* believed him to be," "a restoration which Ulysses himself *never* wished *more heartily,*" "he . . . must have *very* little understanding *indeed,*" "*highly* worthy of censure."[15] These phrases are really standardized signals which are used by Fielding again and again to describe the actions of all characters in all situations. As an inheritor of the eighteenth-entury belief in the universality of human nature, Fielding is at pains to depict his characters not as unique but as representative, an epistemological bias which is reflected in his phraseology: polite, conventional, and thus "low charged." This objective and distant tone is further enforced in this passage by logical adverbs which mark a train of speculation and deduction running through the entire 500 words.

This comparative analysis has thus indicated that Charlotte Brontë uses adverbs with considerable frequency, that syntactically this class occurs often in positions of major stress, that, qualitatively, these adverbs often describe states of mind rather than external areas of time or place, and that they seldom mitigate, but usually intensify the words they modify.

IV

Very generally, it can be said that this stylistic trait contributes to the credibility or lack of credibility of several main characters. Because Brontë's style gives, impressionistically, an

15. Henry Fielding, *Tom Jones* (New York, 1950), pp. 357–358.

effect of heightened emotion recollected in anything but tranquillity by an almost morbidly sensitive female intelligence, this tone is most fitting when it belongs to a Jane Eyre or a Lucy Snowe. Her male narrators are less fortunate, however, for Charlotte Brontë shows little adeptness at tuning her style to a man's emotional range. As a small but important part of the stylistic whole, her way with adverbs can function as a formal indicator of the author's emotional and intellectual grasp of character.

William Crimsworth, the protagonist of Brontë's first novel, *The Professor,* is an example of the author's failure to achieve such a grasp. Kathleen Tillotson has cited the creation of Crimsworth as an example of how complete Charlotte Brontë's detachment and projection had become after the intensely emotional period of her involvement with Constantin Heger.[16] It is more likely, however, that the opposite is true; that Brontë's decision to tell the story of master and pupil in the master's words indicates that she could not yet trust herself to be objective with her own experience, and that Crimsworth represents a deliberate effort to master real feeling. When, years later, she finally has achieved detachment, she can change the title of the narrative from *The Professor* to *Villette,* and use Lucy Snowe successfully to tell the same story. Thus, while the creation of Crimsworth was obviously a psychological necessity, the hero himself is not an artistic success, for Charlotte Brontë shows herself excessively uneasy in the guise of a man, and her greatest genius—an ability to convince us of the emotional intensity of an inner life—falters badly.

Crimsworth is at once too harsh and too feminine, too cold, and too sensitive to convince us, first, of his humanity and, second, of his masculinity. The reader is struck cold immediately by the tone of the letter which opens the novel, an impression which undoubtedly comes from an attempt on the author's part to capture a masculine tone by being excessively "real, cool, and solid." Approaching her effort linguistically, we find that the adverb content of a 500-word passage chosen

16. Kathleen Tillotson, *Novels of the Eighteen-Forties* (Oxford, 1954), pp. 279–280.

at random from chapter 1 is 22—7 fewer than the lowest count
of 29, and 30 lower than the highest of 52 (pp. 2–4: "I wrote . . .
Seacombe"). Of the 22, most are temporal adverbs. Only a few
emotionally intensify the action of the verb, but these are near-
clichés (*mortally* offended, knew *well enough*), and actually
apply to persons other than Crimsworth. Sixteen of the adverbs,
because of position, receive no special stress; in fact, only in the
last sentence of the passage do we hear the familiar rhythm of
Brontë's prose:

> ". . . but as I grew up, and heard by degrees of the persever-
> ing hostility, the hatred till death evinced by them against my
> father—of the sufferings of my mother—of all the wrongs, in
> short, of our house—*then* did I conceive shame of the de-
> pendence in which I lived, and form a resolution *no more* to
> take bread from hands which had refused to minister to the
> necessities of my dying mother."

The scarcity of adverbs in a passage which chills us with its
cool tones can be no coincidence: consciously or unconsciously
Charlotte Brontë is holding back one of her most effective
stylistic cards. In equating masculinity with lack of feeling,
however, she fails to capture our sympathy for Crimsworth, a
sympathy of which he has no need, to judge from his trenchant
description of his mother's death: " 'At the end of the six
months she brought me into the world, and then herself left it,
without, I should think, much regret, as it contained little hope
or comfort for her' " (*P*, p. 3).

On the other hand, Crimsworth is too much at ease in a feminine world to convince us that he can claim a place in the masculine. He is uncomfortably familiar with the most minute
details of feminine occupation and apparel. It is quite unbe-
lievable that any man, let alone one that is motherless and
sisterless, could either know or care that gowns are made of
merino or crepe or stuff, or could ascertain, merely by glancing
across the school room, that it is the netting of a green silk purse
which occupies Mlle. Reuter. Even more unreal, of course, is
Crimsworth's total disdain of feminine beauty and coquetry, an

attitude that is mere wishful thinking on Charlotte Brontë's part. Most unnaturally of all, Crimsworth is possessed of a disturbingly feminine sensibility which allows him to experience frequently some very unlikely sensations, and, even more unnaturally, to comprehend the delicate unfolding of feeling in a member of the opposite sex.

If we examine a page or two that impresses us strongly with Crimsworth's sensitivity rather than his *sangfroid*, it is not surprising that the text contains, instead of 22, 52 adverbs, again confirming that there is a correlation between adverbial modifiers and sentience (pp. 147–148: "Having perused . . . its ardour").[17] The passage is too long to quote in its entirety, but a few lines will serve to show how diction, rhythm, and frequency of qualifying adverbs give the effect of heightened sensibility:

> I put my hand *gently* on her shoulder; no need *further* to prepare her, for she was neither hysterical nor liable to fainting fits; a sudden push, *indeed*, might have startled her, but the contact of my quiet touch *merely* woke attention as I wished; and, though she turned *quickly*, yet *so lightning*-swift is thought —in some minds *especially*—I believe the wonder of what— the consciousness of who it was that *thus* stole unawares on her solitude, had passed through her brain, and flashed into her heart, *even* before she had effected that hasty movement; at least, Amazement had *hardly* opened her eyes and raised them to mine, ere Recognition informed their irids with *most* speaking brightness.

When one realizes that the *action* here occupies at the most a few seconds and could be conveyed by saying, "She looked up as I laid my hand on her shoulder and recognized me almost

17. In the following construction, "a sentiment of most vivid joy shone clear and warm on her whole countenance," *clear* and *warm* may be disputed as adverbs. Brontë very frequently locates words belonging to the adjective-form class in the adverb position after an intransitive verb, thus giving them, I believe, an adverbial function of modifying the verb. This transmutation is further evidence of the significance of adverbs in her prose.

immediately," one realizes the extent to which Charlotte Brontë is concerned with the inner life—with what passes through the brain and flashes into the heart. Her characters do, indeed, feel "in every sentient atom of their frame." When these characters are men, the reader, expecting—perhaps unjustly—a certain masculine reserve or even obtuseness, is apt to find their eloquent perceptiveness suspiciously unreal.

Thus, when Louis Moore in *Shirley* takes out "his little blank book" to "discourse with it" in ardent tones, he reveals himself as still another Brontëan heroine flimsily disguised in waistcoat and spectacles: " 'Her hair was *always* dusk as night, and fine as silk; her neck was *always* fair, flexible, polished—but both have *now* a new charm: the tresses are soft as shadow, the shoulders they fall on wear a goddess-grace. *Once* I *only* SAW her beauty, *now* I FEEL it' " (*S*, p. 482). Besides the poetic *dusk* and *tresses* and the three similes, much of the eloquence is communicated through the heavily stressed adverbs, and again it will come as no surprise to find that 500 words of this rapturous "discourse" contain 46 adverbs (pp. 481–482: "She is . . . morning").

Yet *Shirley's* passionate paean to the titanic mother, Eve, an emotional summit of the novel (which, in a Brontë novel, is saying a good deal), contains in 500 words only 17 adverbs (*S*, pp. 252–253). The eloquence of this outburst is obtained through rhetorical devices common to Victorian prose in general; that is, through rhythms that rise in intensity along heavily parallel clauses, through an abstract and elevated diction, through syntactical inversion and exclamation. The verbs are frequently violent—*flashed, serried, strove, heaved, contend, gushed, sweeps, flame*—a characteristic of language that is more Brontëan than Victorian. The passage, indeed, rises to prophetic frenzy ("I saw—I now see—"); yet, although its sentiments are feministic, its tone is not feminine. The styles of the Moore and Shirley excerpts reflect a typical Brontë inversion of character. Shirley is the masculine force in the Moore-Keeldar relationship (all Shirley's talk of submission is Charlotte's reverse compulsion, grafted unconvincingly on Shirley's masculine temperament), and Louis Moore the femi-

nine: it is Rochester and Jane again, the roles reversed. Or perhaps it would be more accurate to say that characteristically
manly traits of decisiveness, abruptness, vigor, and emotional
strength are given to Shirley, while Moore exhibits the rather
irritable and exaggerated sensibility usually attributed to
women.

In *Jane Eyre* and *Villette*, Charlotte Brontë found the solu-
tion to a problem of characterization she had only partially
resolved in creating Yorke Hunsden and Robert Moore. Hunsden and Robert Moore have about them a convincingly masculine aura because, portrayed from the outside, they are not
under the necessity of revealing their feelings, and, simultaneously, their author's imperfect grasp of them. In a narrative told
by a feminine protagonist, it is far easier to excuse emotional
incongruity on the grounds that, whether or not Rochester or
Emanuel felt thus, Jane and Lucy felt they did. As a matter of
fact, however, there is little that needs to be excused about
either character.

Rochester, with his tall horse, great dog, "full falcon-eye,"
mad wife, and manor house, can share the palm with Fitzwil-
liam Darcy as the ultimate creation of feminine wishful thinking. Yet his sensuality and good-humored bluntness of manner
vivify him, and the character succeeds where the finicking and
arrogant Crimsworth and Moore fail. As suggested before, this
success is chiefly due to the novel's point of view; other formal
devices, however, contribute to Rochester's credibility. One of
these worth noting here is a method of distancing achieved by
what can be described as direct indirect discourse. The occasion is the playing and singing of a love ballad. When, immediately following, Rochester rises impetuously and strides toward
Jane, "his face all kindled and his full falcon-eye flashing," the
ensuing dialogue is reported in a form which employs the third
person, yet omits the indirect discourse signal: ". . . I asked
with asperity, 'whom he was going to marry now?' 'That was
a strange question to be put by his darling Jane'" (*JE*, p. 259).
Jane at this point wishes to quench all demonstrations of feeling; the form holds Rochester off at arm's length as effectively
as Jane's tartness.

Rochester's voice is usually directly heard, however; and although he is on-stage a great deal and has many long speeches, his accents are sufficiently manly to be convincing. Two passages selected at random indicate why this is so (pp. 135–136: "And Miss Eyre . . . you have"; pp. 289–290: "Well, Jane . . . in a"). The two samples contain 34 and 28 adverbs, a comparatively low number in Brontëan prose, yet significantly more than occurred in Crimsworth's letter. Of these, however, many are "neutral": *meantime, alternately, also, now, there,* etc. Both passages are narratives, and it occurs to us that much—perhaps most—of Rochester's talk is given over to describing for Jane (and us) events in his past which explain the present. Unlike Brontë heroines, much of the time Rochester is capable of objectivity: he can judge himself as occasionally ridiculous and report his weaknesses with irony. In this ironic context, many normally intensifying adverbs become comic:

> "And, Miss Eyre, *so much* was I flattered by this preference of the Gallic sylph for her British gnome . . . . I sat down in her boudoir; happy to breathe the air consecrated *so lately* by her presence. No,—I exaggerate; I *never* thought there was any consecrating virtue about her: it was *rather* a sort of pastille perfume . . . ." (*JE,* p. 135)

In moments like this, when Rochester can ridicule in the next breath the sensibility he has shown in the last, Charlotte Brontë shows that she has achieved stylistically a more realistic grasp of character.

Paul Emanuel is especially successful, emanating from his ugly and vigorous person some of the strange but tangible sexual vitality of Shakespeare's Richard III and Dickens's Quilp, both of whom are capable of calling forth violent reactions from women, whether of hate or love. Yet Charlotte Brontë uses a great deal of stylistic restraint in depicting M. Paul. He has moments of great tenderness ("'Bonne petite amie!' said he softly; 'douce consolatrice!'"), but they are few, restrained, and believable. He has moments of great rage and sorrow, but they are portrayed less through rhetoric than through external action which in turn is reported with a spirited and critical objectivity by Lucy Snowe.

All the agony of the almost-thwarted love affair is Lucy's: "Morning wasted. Afternoon came, and I thought all was over. My heart trembled in its place. My blood was troubled in its current. I was quite sick, and hardly knew how to keep at my post or do my work" (V, p. 374). From Lucy, these sentiments and the form they are couched in are genuinely affecting; had either been Emanuel's they would not have rung true. Realistically, while Lucy is agonizing in suspense, Emanuel is proceeding off-scene with quiet, masculine practicality to secure both their futures. This deliberate under-exposure of character is partially responsible for its success: M. Paul strides in and out of the *pensionnat,* he descends to rail in a whirlwind of passion and as quickly retreats, he plays the kind benefactor while the *pensionnat* sleeps. What we know of him is believable; what we do not adds to rather than detracts from the reality.

This distancing is further achieved by several devices of style or form. Unlike Rochester, Emanuel is given no long speeches. Much of the dialogue he is given is reported in French, a practice which obscures rather than illuminates his sentiments for most readers. And then, some of Emanuel's most intimate words to Lucy are reported in indirect discourse form, so that while the sentiment is his, the prose rhythms, the diction—the form, in short—is Lucy's:

> He asked, by-and-by, if I would not rather run to my companions than sit there? . . . He asked whether, if I were his sister, I should always be content to stay with a brother such as he. . . . Again, he inquired whether, if he were to leave Villette, and go far away, I should be sorry . . . . I hid my face with the book, for it was covered with tears. I asked him why he talked so; and he said he would talk so no more . . . .
> (p. 324)

Must one conclude that the frequent or emphatic use of adverbs is somehow characteristic of a feminine style? This conclusion is far too sweeping. Undoubtedly, the conspicuous presence of a grammatical class which functions to describe and shade verbs, adjectives, and other adverbs indicates in a writer an awareness of the many-faceted nature of experience. Traditionally, women have been considered more qualitative than men, tending to take an interest in the diverse and subtle ramifications of action, while in men there is a tendency to see life more steadily and see it whole. But then one thinks of Henry James, and, in a different way, of Thomas Hardy and D. H. Lawrence. Perhaps the most that can be said is that a particular stress laid upon this vehicle of expression is evidence of a special concern with interior instead of exterior action. For this reason, one can hypothesize that adverbial frequency will generally be a characteristic of narrative rather than of expository writing, and of the narrative of sensibility rather than the narrative of action and adventure.

In an age of great exuberance and extrovertism, in an age dedicated to the ideal of action rather than contemplation, it is not surprising that Charlotte Brontë's prose should exhibit a stylistic trait which reflects a mind alienated from these pursuits; which singles her out as a writer who is dedicated rather to describing the emotions "felt in the heart and felt along the blood" of the alienated and passionate soul.

2

SYNTACTIC INVERSION

POETIC AND PERVERSE

Among the ample and elaborate cadences of Victorian prose, Charlotte Brontë's narrative style stands apart for its prevailing effect of brevity, vigor, and swiftness. If we examine a typical paragraph from *Villette*, the syntactical causes of this effect become clear:

> Twilight had passed into night, and the lamps were lit in the streets, ere I issued from that sombre church. To turn back was now become possible to me; the wild longing to breathe this October wind on the little hill far without the city-walls had ceased to be an imperative impulse, and was softened into a wish with which Reason could cope: she put it down, and I turned, as I thought, to the Rue Fossette. But I had become involved in a part of the city with which I was not familiar; it was the old part, and full of narrow streets of picturesque, ancient, and mouldering houses. I was much too weak to be very collected, and I was still too careless of my own welfare and safety, to be cautious. I grew embarrassed; I got immeshed in a net-work of turns unknown. I was lost, and had no resolution to ask guidance of any passenger.
>
> If the storm had lulled a little at sunset, it made up now for

lost time. Strong and horizontal thundered the current of the wind from north-west to south-east; it brought rain like spray, and sometimes, a sharp hail like shot; it was cold and pierced me to the vitals. I bent my head to meet it, but it beat me back. My heart did not fail at all in this conflict; I only wished that I had wings and could ascend the gale, spread and repose my pinions on its strength, career in its course, sweep where it swept. (V, p. 141)

Content apart, it will be readily noted that the swift pace of this passage derives not from short sentences (there are only three), but from the effect of short sentences created by twenty-one independent clauses within nine sentences.[1] When conjunctions are used they are predominantly coordinating conjunctions that further contribute to the short-clause effect, as do the frequent compound predicates. The result of these paratactic constructions is a prose of action, uncomplicated by speculation, ramification, qualification, or parenthesis. We are constantly confronted by subject and verb, and, significantly, by more verbs than subjects: thirty-six verbs to twenty-eight subjects, not counting seven infinitive phrases. It comes as a surprise to find that much of this action is internal, dealing with longing or wishing, or the state of being collected, careless, or embarrassed. But in Brontë's prose even thought is dramatized, concretized, and externalized, often literally, by the device of personification: "I bent my head: I sat thinking an hour longer. Reason still whispered me, laying on my shoulder a withered hand, and frostily touching my ear with the chill blue lips of eld" (V, p. 196).

Charlotte Brontë uses more punctuation, according to my count, than do Austen, Emily Brontë, Thackeray, Eliot, or

1. Of course, the pace is not always swift. In *Shirley* particularly there is a good deal of rather laboriously speculative and opinionizing talk. But at its best, Brontë's prose has animation and speed: "Without being allowed time or power to deliberate, I found myself in the same breath convoyed along as in a species of whirlwind, up stairs, up two pair of stairs, nay, actually up three (for this fiery little man seemed as by instinct to know his way everywhere); to the solitary and lofty attic was I borne, put in and locked in, the key being on the door, and that key he took with him, and vanished" (V, p. 115).

Dickens; particularly, because her prose is composed of many independent clauses strung together, she uses more colons and semicolons than any of these writers.[2] One critic has speculated that a writer's use of punctuation can provide us with a clue to his psychology; but aside from telling us that Scott uses many commas and few colons, that Thackeray avoids exclamation marks and courts the semicolon, and that Dickens uses few colons, his study disappointingly fails to tell us how these "punctuation profiles" are revealing of personality.[3] Without pressing the matter too far, one can find, I believe, that Brontë's punctuation (and, more significantly, the sentence structure that creates it) reveals and confirms certain elements of her prose, her fiction, and her world-view.

The relatively short series of independent clauses in combination with first-person narrative effectively keeps the subject/author—the "I"—constantly before the reader. The result, of course, is a subjective prose, heavily concentrated upon the immediate sensations of the narrator, with little latitude permitted for looking about, so to speak: for speculation, for philosophizing, or qualification. The result equally is an insistent prose, a prose at an opposite pole from the style of Henry James, characterized mischievously by G. K. Chesterton as "The Hampered, or Obstacle Race Style, in which one continually trips over commas and relative clauses; and where the sense has to be perpetually qualified lest it should mean too much." At an opposite pole, too, are the painfully obscure narrations of

2. In six randomly selected narrative passages of one thousand words from the four novels, Brontë uses 167, 159, 145, 148, 189, and 162 marks of punctuation. This is considerably more than 105, 134, and 126 in similar passages from *Mansfield Park* and *Persuasion;* 131 and 131 in two passages from *Vanity Fair;* 92, 105, 84 from *Middlemarch;* 131 in *David Copperfield,* 116 in *Martin Chuzzlewit,* 126 in *Great Expectations,* and 130 in *Pickwick Papers.* Although one cannot determine whether some of the punctuation is editorial rather than original, the pattern that emerges is undoubtedly valid.

3. E. L. Thorndike, "The Psychology of Punctuation," *American Journal of Psychology* 61 (1948): 222–228. See also Walker Gibson's punctuation criteria for distinguishing "tough," "sweet," and "stuffy" styles: *Tough, Sweet and Stuffy* (Bloomington, Ind., 1966).

Conrad's Marlow, a man constantly grappling with the impossibility of conveying the accurate impression or the real circumstance. We feel that Marlow, inheritor of all the uncertainties of the post-Victorian world, is reluctant to tell; we know that Brontë's protagonists *must*. The many colons, indicative of illustration and example, the coordinate clauses and compound predicates studded with *ands* and *buts,* give to Brontë's prose a Biblical weight and directness, consonant both with the necessity of her style and the frequently didactic tenor of her novels. Finally, the close series of independent clauses, heavily punctuated, impose upon Brontë's style a feeling of restraint. For prose to be emotive, it has often been observed, it must be written with long, sustained rhythms. While the adverb lends an emotive quality to Brontë's prose, this quality is countered—checked, bridled, and disciplined—by barriers of semicolons, colons, and periods. Sentence structure enforces a stringency that the adverb frequently denies, and tension is generated from these conflicting parts.

Characteristic as these series of short clauses with their heavy punctuation may be, they are not, I believe, the most significant (or "foregrounded," to adapt Mukarovsky's term) aspect of Charlotte Brontë's syntax, nor the topic to be considered here. More important is the author's use of syntactic inversion.

Although inversion is not common to prose statement, all novelists use inversion. In the following passage from *Little Dorrit,* Dickens employs the device humorously to exaggerate the splendor of the Merdle equipage and seriously, by placing the descriptive adjectives before the telling verb *looked,* to emphasize syntactically that this splendor is mere external sham: "Bright the carriage looked, sleek the horses looked, gleaming the harness looked, luscious and lasting the liveries looked." But one can read pages of Dickens without coming across this particular device; it is rarer in Austen, and extremely infrequent in Eliot and Thackeray. On the other hand, as the following passage from *Villette* so aptly illustrates, inversion may be regarded as one of the signatures of Charlotte Brontë's style:

Some fearful hours went over me: indescribably was I torn,

racked and oppressed in mind . . . galled was my inmost spirit with an unutterable sense of despair about the future. Motive there was none why I should try to recover or wish to live; and yet quite unendurable was the pitiless and haughty voice in which Death challenged me to engage his unknown terrors. When I tried to pray I could only utter these words:—

"From my youth up Thy terrors have I suffered with a troubled mind."

Most true was it. (*V*, pp. 137–138)

Three types of inversion occur most frequently in the novels: (1) predicate plus subject, (2) noun plus adjective, and (3) object or complement plus subject and predicate.[4] Of the first type—P + S—it will be useful to distinguish two types of constructions: predicate adverb plus predicate plus subject, and predicate adjective plus predicate plus subject. The following examples of PAdv + P + S (or S + P) are randomly chosen and typical:

Scarcely dared I answer her . . . . (*JE*, p. 19)

Under the trees of this cemetery nestled a warm breathless gloom . . . . (*P*, p. 147)

"Willingly would I have observed her last wish . . . ." (*P*, p. 150)

Perhaps, in these incompatibilities of the "physique" with the "morale," lay the secret of that fitful gloom . . . . (*P*, p. 27)

Down washed the rain, deep lowered the welkin . . . . (*V*, p. 329)

Already the cold sweat started on my brow, already I glanced back over my shoulder . . . . (*P*, p. 61)

4. Strictly speaking, the term *inversion* is commonly used only for the placing of the subject after the verb. The term *transposed* is frequently used for constructions in which the object is moved up before the subject and the verb: Stuart Robertson and Frederic G. Cassidy, *The Development of Modern English*, 2d ed. (Englewood Cliffs, New Jersey, 1963), p. 286. To avoid confusion in terminology, however, and following the example of Kames, Whately, and Spencer, I have used the word inversion to describe syntactic structures which depart from common English word order.

Not so had I bid the boys at Pelet's take their reading-books. (*P*, p. 71)

All that night did I ask myself these questions . . . . (*P*, p. 31)

Well did I remember Mrs. Reed's face . . . . (*JE*, p. 218)

Because the adverb complement is syntactically flexible, inversions like these are the least startling instances of the device in Charlotte Brontë's prose. If an actual survey of inversion types were made, almost certainly the Padv + P + S would be found to crop up most frequently. In some cases, of course, this inverted order is normal idiomatic English: *Here are the answers,* or *Never say die.* Perhaps it is the presence of such constructions in the language that conditions an English speaker to accept as comparatively everyday literary language a construction like "In this trait lay the answer." In Charlotte Brontë's prose, however, this particular inversion is persistent enough to command our attention, and often recherché enough to decidedly startle us, if not with a locution like "Sharp and short I turned around; fast I retraced my steps," then with the pyrotechnics of the following: "Up the blood rushed to his face; forth flashed the fire from his eyes; erect he sprang; he held his arms out; but I evaded the embrace, and at once quitted the room" (*JE*, pp. 302–303).

The second type of P + S inversion—PAdj + P + S (or S + P) —is far less common in speech and in prose. The reason may well lie in the semantic difficulties occasioned by locating a qualifier so many positions away from its noun in a construction where unexpected order already provides a momentary check to clarity. In the clause "Close to my elbow was the directress," the adverb complement is, after all, still adjacent to its verb, so that despite the unexpected word order, there is no difficulty in mentally hooking up the adverb with its verb. In a locution like "Sweet could be her smile," however, the reader has to make a certain effort to connect *sweet* with *smile,* four slots away. In poetry, the inversion is more common, and we therefore absorb the construction with less shock: "Vain are the thousand creeds / That move men's hearts, unutterably vain . . . ."

In prose, however, and particularly in eighteenth- and mid-nineteenth-century English prose fiction, which we expect because of its predominantly realistic and social bent to be straightforward, such decidedly unprosaic constructions are startling. Such is their impact in Brontë's novels. While some of the effect of this inversion is lost out of context, it is worthwhile to cite a few examples. Sometimes we are put to task by a contortion like "tawny he himself well knew that it was"(*V*, p. 15); more typical are:

Grave as usual, almost sombre, was her face . . . . (*P*, p. 118)

"Different, indeed," she concluded, "is Robert's mental condition to mine . . . ." (*S*, p. 136)

Her eyes, whose colour I had not at first known, so dim were they with repressed tears, so shadowed with ceaseless dejection . . . . (*P*, p. 130)

Boistrous was the welcome given by the stewardess to "the Watsons" . . . . (*V*, p. 44)

. . . well-arranged was her simple attire, smooth her dark hair, orderly her tranquil room . . . . (*P*, p. 192)

Or here is Shirley's Fieldhead:

Very sombre it was; long, vast, and dark . . . . The gallery on high, opposite the entrance, was seen but in outline, *so shadowy became this hall* towards its ceiling . . . . *Very handsome,* reader, *these shining brown panels are: very mellow in colouring and tasteful in effect* . . . . (*S*, pp. 154–155)

An inversion still more uncommon to prose is the noun plus adjective inversion. Yet it is frequent in Brontë's prose:

. . . I mused on its contents for a few moments—whether with sentiments pleasurable or otherwise I will hereafter note . . . . It was directed in a hand to me unknown—small, and rather neat . . . . (*P*, p. 170)

. . . a flame, as genial as still, as pure as quenchless . . . .
(*P*, p. 149)

. . . to teach young ladies would be an occupation so interesting . . . an incident so new . . . . (*P*, p. 64)

. . . they were the impressions of an ignorance crasse. (*V*,
p. 185)

. . . a clearness of skin almost bloom, and a plumpness almost
embonpoint . . . . (*P*, p. 130)

. . . at last, came a tone accordant, an echo responsive . . . .
(*V*, p. 357)

The N + A construction is particularly conspicuous in *Jane
Eyre*, where it is used either in description of nature or of people: "clouds so sombre, and a rain so penetrating"; "cornfields
forest-high"; "clouds, low and livid"; "a cormorant, dark and
large"; "her disk, silver-white and crystal-clear"; "tears, hot and
large"; "a figure . . . broad-chested and thin flanked"; "an eye
hollow and fixed"; "a brow quite bloodless"; "a demonic laugh
—low, suppressed and deep."

Stephen Ullmann has analyzed the semantic nuances available to the writer of French because of the mobility of the
adjective in that language. It is possible, for example, to differentiate between subjective and objective attitudes: an adjective in pre-noun position implies emotional participation; an
adjective in post-noun position implies an objective, factual, or
rational attitude. *Une découverte importante* is thus a statement
of fact; *une importante découverte* an emotive utterance.[5] In
English, the fixed pre-noun position of the adjective makes its
inversion a matter of style rather than meaning. Only rarely in
speech does the adjective follow the noun and when it does,
the construction is so unusual that the native speaker usually
refuses to acknowledge it, with the result that the adjective
becomes absorbed into the nominative as a whole. This is the
case, for example, in a borrowing like *court martial*, in French

5. Stephen Ullmann, *Style in the French Novel* (Cambridge, Eng.,
1957), p. 7.

a noun plus adjective, but in English a compound noun; or in a proper compound noun like *Highland Park West*. This rarity is responsible for the strain one feels in this Brontëan arrangement: "A *lover masculine* so disappointed can speak and urge explanation; a *lover feminine* can say nothing . . ." (S, p. 81). As Otto Jespersen has pointed out, the only really important exception to the N + A order in English occurs when there are qualifications added to the adjective "which draw it after the noun so that the whole complex serves the purpose of a relative clause"; he cites from Stevenson, "an interruption too brief and isolated to attract more notice."[6] The N + A inversion is too forced even for Charlotte Brontë (note examples above); she frequently tempers this construction by doubling the adjective (*low and livid*) or inserting an adverb (a brow *quite* bloodless) so that the effect is closer to that of a relative clause. It is interesting that the post-noun position of the adjective in English suggests emotional involvement, just the opposite of its meaning in French.

Finally, there occur in the novels a great many constructions in which the direct object (or noun complement), normally found after the verb, initiates the sentence. Often these clauses involve a double inversion since the subject is relegated to a post-verb position: "Ornaments had she none," for example. In this inversion category may be included cases where the indirect object occurs in an unexpected position. Because of the greater mobility of the indirect object, these inversions are less striking; yet it will be agreed that the syntax of a sentence like "He gave to me the pen" is wrenched into an order more common to German or French than to English. Although this type of word order is often used by the French characters in the novels when speaking English, it is by no means limited to their speech. The following are representative of the O + S + P:

> Something of vengeance I had tasted for the first time . . . .
> (*JE*, p. 37)

---

6. Otto Jespersen, *Growth and Structure of the English Language*, 9th ed. (New York, 1938), p. 11.

Her look of affright I answered with one of composure . . . .
(*P*, p. 87)

John, no one thwarted, much less punished . . . . (*JE*, p. 15)

. . . an immutable purpose that eye spoke . . . . (*V*, p. 59)

. . . small English features they all possess . . . . (*S*, p. 118)

Liberty I clasped in my arms for the first time . . . . (*P*, p. 46)

Me, she had dispensed from joining the group . . . . (*JE*, p. 7)

. . . over one she had acquired power by her skilful management
of his bad temper; over another by little attentions to his petty
caprices; a third she had subdued by flattery; a fourth—a timid
man—she kept in awe by a sort of austere decision of mien; me,
she still watched, still tried by the most ingenious tests . . . .
(*P*, p. 90)

All the inversions cited so far have one thing in common:
they are all matters of style in which ordinary sentence order
has arbitrarily been put aside for less common syntactical structures. There are a group of sentence inversions in English, however, in which—to use H. W. Fowler's phrase—"inversion itself
serves a purpose." This group includes interrogative, imperative, exclamatory, and hypothetical sentences. Fowler states
that inversion in these constructions is the "natural," though by
no means invariable practice.[7] If inversion here is "natural,"
one could argue that the only stylistic significance of such constructions must lie in the frequency with which an author employs them. This, however, is not really the case.

Take the hypothetical statement. It is as possible to write
If I had known this as *Had I known this.* Similarly, the construction *If I were in command of the situation* is as likely as
the inverted *Were I in command of the situation.* Thus it is stylistically significant that Charlotte Brontë usually chooses the
inverted form when writing in the first person (*Had I known*),
and often extends the preference to a third person construction:
"If there is no change—if there dawns no prospect of peace

7. H. W. Fowler, *A Dictionary of Modern English Usage,* 2d ed., re-
vised by Sir Ernest Gowers (New York, 1965), p. 296.

. . . ." (S, p. 129). Similarly, an inversion choice exists in the verb order of an exclamatory sentence: one can say *How meaningless is life!* or *How meaningless life is!*—the latter is more common, less rhetorical. Even here Charlotte Brontë, unlike many writers, is decidedly inclined to reverse the natural order of things:

> What a consternation of soul was mine . . . . (*JE*, p. 15)
>
> Yet in what darkness, what dense ignorance, was the mental battle fought! (*JE*, p. 15)
>
> How thankful was I to be able to answer with truth . . . . (*V*, p. 53)
>
> How fast beat every pulse in my frame! (*V*, p. 55)
>
> . . . how precious seems one shrub, how lovely an enclosed and planted spot of ground! (*V*, p. 90)

Questions and commands involve inversion so commonly that their significance must lie almost wholly in the frequency with which they occur, although it would be a matter of interest if an author invariably wrote *You are going?*, *You know him?*, and so forth.[8] Without resorting to comparative counts, it can be said with some certainty that Brontë's novels contain an unusual number of commands and interrogations. Content provides an explanation. Brontë novels are peopled with brusque, domineering characters and rife with situations in which these characters —directors, masters, teachers, *maîtresses*, gentlemen, heiresses —are called upon to exercise authority over subordinates:

8. Imperatives, of course, do not usually involve placing the verb before the subject, but dropping the subject altogether. Since they are included in Fowler's *Dictionary of Modern English Usage,* I have included them here. Richard Ohmann has found that Victorian differs from eighteenth-century prose on three counts: Victorians use more questions and imperatives; they use the transformation that converts nouns into adjectives less frequently; and they incorporate more basic sentences with intransitive verbs. See his "A Linguistic Appraisal of Victorian Style," in *The Art of Victorian Prose,* ed. George Levine and William Madden (London, 1968), pp. 289–313. Undoubtedly the rhetorical and didactic nature of Victorian prose primarily accounts for the quantity of questions and imperatives.

hence the occasion for a more than ordinary number of imperatives. Examples abound: Crimsworth, Louis Moore, M. Paul, and Lucy in the schoolroom; Jane as a subordinate in her relationship with the Reeds, Brocklehurst, Rochester, and St. John Rivers; Blanche Ingram's imperiousness; the meek Caroline Helstone taking orders from her uncle, from Hortense, and even from Robert; Shirley herself, pleasantly dominating everyone. The number of interrogatives also stems in part from the authoritarian brusqueness of characters who seldom think it an impertinence to query directly: one thinks of Jane quizzed by Brocklehurst. More responsible for the frequent questions, however, is the isolation of so many principal characters. Characters who are firmly lodged within a family, or within a circle of friends, or even in a town are not likely to ask a great many questions: they know and are known. Brontë's protagonists, however, are without family, frequently without friends, often without permanent residence. When they encounter another character, it is as though each has emerged from a void: neither has had previous information about the other, or at best very little. This circumstance generates the many extended episodes of question and answer in the novels: Jane quizzing Helen Burns about Lowood or her family; Rochester examining Adèle's new governess; Jane querying Rochester about his past; St. John Rivers interrogating the runaway Jane—to cite only instances from *Jane Eyre*. Isolation also gives rise to frequent soliloquy and soliloquy to "the ceaseless inward question": we think of Caroline's lonely brooding over her unrequited love, or Jane's despairing query: "Why do I struggle to retain a valueless life?"

One other type of inversion deserves notice, and that is the P + S inversion in speech tags. Frequently inversion is preferable: *"Please do," answered the directress* is more satisfying than *"Please do," the directress answered*. Often the choice is a matter of indifference: the appearance of *said he* is undoubtedly dictated by the writer's boredom with *he said*. The function of the speech tag is simply to distinguish the speaker (and perhaps something about the circumstances of his speech), and should not call attention to itself. As long as common verbs like *said, replied,* or *answered* are involved, inversion is usually inconspicuous. When, however, variants and expansions of these verbs are inverted, the dialogue frame can become as conspicuous as the dialogue it signals: compare *I reflected* with *reflected I.* From what we have already discovered about Charlotte Brontë's penchant for inversion, we will not be surprised to find that her novels contain a great many dialogue frames which jolt us because of the P + S construction:

> "Good evening, Mr. Hunsden," muttered I with a bow . . . . (*P*, p. 18)
>
> "Clerk and shopman!" murmured I to myself. (*P*, p. 49)
>
> "Commencez!" cried I . . . . (*P*, p. 52)
>
> "Des bêtes de somme,—des bêtes de somme," murmured scornfully the director. (*P*, p. 78)
>
> "I black my boots," pursued he, savagely. (*V*, p. 342)
>
> "I don't blush—I never DO blush," affirmed she . . . . (*V*, p. 363)
>
> "Bien, bien!" interrupted I . . . . (*P*, p. 63)

Brontë is also fond of a construction which is not strictly inversion since subject and complement are equal grammatical entities and reversible, but in which she frequently positions the most logical initial element last: *No inn was this* is an example. This construction occurs most frequently in speech tags, with an "inverted" effect:

> "I should indeed like to go to school," was the audible conclusion of my musings. (*JE*, p. 25)
>
> "Of course, I know he will marry Shirley," were her first words when she rose in the morning. (*S*, p. 204)
>
> "But I shall be forgotten when they ARE married," was the cruel succeeding thought. (*S*, p. 204)

All authors use inversion in speech tags; Charlotte Brontë's predilection for wry syntax leads her to use it flagrantly, so that the reader's attention is constantly drawn to the frame.

The many functional inversions, the inverted speech tags, and the optional stylistic inversions cited above all serve to make this syntactic idiosyncracy one of the most characteristic traits of Charlotte Brontë's style. No attempt has been made to arrive at the actual percentage of inverted sentences in her fiction, but a count of the device as it occurs in four chapters chosen at random can help give us an idea of the ratio: chapter 2 of *Jane Eyre:* 115 sentences, 65 containing inversion, over 50 percent; chapter 9 of *Shirley* (pp. 112–122): 160 sentences, 50 containing inversion; approximately 33 percent; chapter 7 of *Villette*: 178 sentences, 62 containing inversion, approximately 33 per cent; chapter 20 of *The Professor*: 81 sentences, 17 containing inversion, approximately 20 percent.[9] If we can take the part to be indicative of the whole, then only about 66 percent of Charlotte Brontë's sentences are cast entirely in the common S-V-O order. This ratio becomes striking when compared with the percentage of S-V-O sentences in other prose writers. Jespersen and F. J. Curtis have provided some statistics: Macaulay, 82 percent; Carlyle, 87; Shelley (prose), 89; Dickens, 91; Byron (prose), 93; Milton (prose), the Bible, and Meredith, 94; Kipling (prose), Thackeray, and H. G. Wells, 95; Pinero, 97; Ruskin, 98; Darwin, 99.1; Shaw, 99.8.[10] If, as Ullmann states,

9. As indicated above, Charlotte Brontë's sentences consist chiefly of many independent clauses strung together with either semicolons or colons. Of all the clauses, one clause may be inverted, the rest in common order. Since it seemed practical to count sentences rather than independent clauses, I have counted as inverted those sentences containing one or more inversions as against those which contain no inversion at all. I have also numbered among the inverted those sentences of dialogue which are signaled by inverted speech tags. Thus a construction like, " 'You are right,' returned I," counts as an inversion.

10. Jespersen, *Growth and Structure,* p. 11; F. J. Curtis, "*Sprache und Literatur:* A Review of Henry Bradley's *The Making of Literature* (London, 1904) and Jespersen's *Growth and Structure of the English Language* (Leipzig, 1905)," *Beiblatt zur Anglia* 19 (May 1908): 129–142. Unfortunately, neither Jespersen nor Curtis tells us how these figures were reached: whether, for example, dialogue was included in the novels, or how sentences containing more than one inversion were counted (see my footnote 9 above). Jespersen gives us this account: "A few years ago, I made my pupils calculate statistically various points in regard to word

"the effective force of the device depends in no small measure on whether it deviates from normative usage," we may reckon that inversion in Brontë's novels is forceful indeed.[11]

But according to rhetorical principles, deviation from normative usage is not the only reason for the force of inversion in Brontë's prose. Herbert Spencer, speaking from a utilitarian point of view in his *Philosophy of Style* (1883), theorizes that inversion is the more forceful, economic, and effective mode of expression because it is logically clearer. Citing the well-worn example, "Great is Diana of the Ephesians," he asserts that the superiority of this construction to "Diana of the Ephesians is great" lies in the fact that the meaning-bearing predicate occurs first, so that the mind is "led directly, and without error, to the intended impression." But Spencer here is only reiterating what rhetoricians like Whately, Blair, Campbell, and Kames stipulated before him. According to Kames's *Elements of Criticism:* "In the arrangement of *predicate and subject,* for example, we are at once shown that as the predicate determines the aspect under which the subject is to be conceived, it should be placed first; and the striking effect produced by so placing it becomes comprehensible." The habitual use of sentences in which limiting or descriptive elements precede those described or limited is called *inverted style,* but should be called, says Kames (confusingly enough), the *direct style* because of its superior clarity, economy, and force.

But the inverted style gathers force from another source. Indirectly, say Kames, Whately, and Spencer, inversion is associated in the reader's mind with the spontaneous form of mental excitement. An angry man does not say, "He shall go out," but *"Out with him!"* or *"Away with him!"* A child, describing a make-believe shoot-out, does not cry, "The gun went

---

order in different languages. I give here only the percentages in some modern authors of sentences in which the subject preceded the verb, and the latter in turn preceded its object (as in 'I saw him' as against 'Him I saw, but not her' or 'Whom did you see?')," (*Growth and Structure,* p. 11). The percentages are thus offered for what they are worth, although undoubtedly different criteria were used than mine.

11. Ullmann, *Style in the French Novel,* p. 6.

bang," but *"Bang went the gun!"* Of a distressing occasion, one is apt to exclaim, *"Never was I so embarrassed!"* "The emotions," says Kames, "that have from time to time been produced by the strong thoughts wrapped up in these forms, are partially aroused by the forms themselves. They create a certain degree of animation; they induce a preparatory sympathy; and when the striking ideas looked for are reached, they are the more vividly realized."[12]

It is significant that the examples of inverted style cited by these rhetoricians are virtually all drawn from poetry. The explanation is obvious: despite all theorizing about what *should* be the ideal form of prose expression, in fact inversion is a characteristic of poetry rather than prose. Critics have been fond of asserting that the Brontës brought "poetry" to the English novel and not elaborating further, perhaps because by poetry is meant subjectivity or "feeling," and it is all too obvious that the content of Charlotte Brontë's novels contains a good deal of that article. But this amorphous poetic quality is largely a matter of form. If the burden of feeling may be carried by an apparently minor stylistic entity like the adverb (as the first chapter endeavored to show), how much more of the burden rests upon the major rhetorical device of syntactical inversion. Jespersen has cited the straightforward subject-verb-object syntax as a principal contributor to the masculine character of the English language. Is inverted prose feminine? Or is it not rather evocative of the heightened emotional drama we associate with poetry?

12. Herbert Spencer, *Philosophy of Style* (New York, 1917), pp. 18–19; Lord Henry Kames, *Elements of Criticism* (New York, 1877), pp. 426, 436–437; Richard Whately, *Elements of Rhetoric,* ed. Douglas Ehninger (Carbondale, Ill., 1963), pp. 312–316. DeQuincey in his "Rhetoric," however, observes that the correct order places the agent first, then the act, and finally the object: see *The Collected Works of Thomas de Quincey,* ed. David Masson, Vol. 10 (Edinburgh, 1890), pp. 96–99. The idea that English *should* conform to a certain order is, of course, foreign to modern linguistic thought, which simply observes that more than 80 percent of English sentences *are* cast in a subject-verb-object order. Spencer, Whately, and Kames are themselves forced to admit finally that the predicate-subject order is too forceful and must be used sparingly.

For inversion provides, primarily, unusual emphasis. One source of this emphasis is simply tactical: the unexpected occurrence of a word(s) in the most prominent part of a sentence —the beginning: "*Liberty* I clasped in my arms." (Note too that capitalization contributes to prominence.) Another source of emphasis lies in stress, for all inversion involves the manipulation of key words or phrases into positions of heavy accent. Brontë is especially adept here; compare "fòrệst-hígh córn-fièlds" / "córnfièlds fórẽst-hígh"; or "ā sòft, swèet sóuthwìnd" / "ā sóuthwìnd, sóft ānd swéet."

Emphasis and the rhythmic patterns it sets in motion stimulates a heightened emotional response from the reader. Part of this response, of course, derives from the quality of the word(s) chosen for prominence. It is interesting—perhaps inevitable—that the elements Charlotte Brontë chooses most frequently to stress are themselves closely allied to poetry: the descriptive and the subjective. The descriptive effect achieved by such constructions as *Long did the hours seem* or *So sweet were the tones* needs no comment. Some examples may elucidate, however, the various syntactic manipulations Charlotte Brontë uses to bring the narrator into the spotlight:

It was directed in a hand *to me* unknown . . . . (P, p. 170)

To me, once or twice, she had . . . uttered venturous thoughts . . . . (*P*, p. 210)

Me, she had dispensed from joining the group . . . . (*JE*, p. 7)

The post had, indeed, arrived; *by me* unheard. (*V*, p. 232)

Perhaps most subjective emphasis is achieved by the inverted speech tags where stress is transferred from the verb to the pronoun. Compare: " 'Clérk ānd shópmàn!' Ì múrmùred," with " 'Clérk ānd shópmàn!' múrmùred Ì." E. M. Forster has claimed that "the whole intricate question of method . . . resolves itself not into formulae but into the power of the writer to bounce the reader into accepting what he says."[13] When readers exclaim about the passion, the power, and the poetry of Charlotte

---

13. E. M. Forster, *Aspects of the Novel* (New York, 1954), pp. 79–80.

Brontë's novels, they are responding in no small degree to being "bounced" by her practice of reversing the common orders of prose.

II

But inversion creates another effect even more characteristic of the novels than the poetic, and even more intrinsically linked to the content of the fiction, and ultimately, I believe, to its creator's personality. This quality can best be defined as a pervasive tension: Charlotte Brontë's prose is simply never at rest. This sense of strain arises in part from contradictions in tone—the too frequent unholy alliance of morality and passion, for example. Most responsible for the tension, however, is the inverted syntax: whatever rhetoricians claim is the ideal form of prose, they are forced to admit finally that inversion is neither common to prose, nor is its frequent use desirable, since the rarity of the form—and hence, its difficulty—creates a sense of strain in the mind of the reader. And this is one effect of inversion in Brontë's novels: when a reader is brought up short five or six times per page by finding words where he least expected them, the result must be a sense of disquiet. The tension of Brontë's style undoubtedly reflects the tensions of its creator. But since style is choice, one can go further, I believe, and identify in Brontë's deliberate and flagrant practice of inverting the normal order of the English language not only a poetic sense, but a taste for distortion, a certain contrariness, a delight in negativeness and reversal that can be called perverse.[14] And these qualities are apparent not only in the formal aspects of her prose, but in the content of her fiction as well: no other Victorian writer has created in so few novels so many characters who possess "at their heart's core" a negative delight in going against the grain. This does not mean, of course, that these

14. Charlotte Brontë herself frequently uses the word *perverse* to describe her characters' behavior. See, for example, *P*, pp. 40, 216; *S*, pp. 397, 417, 463, 479; *V*, pp. 77, 84, 161, 281, 288, 325.

characters are unrealistic or even exaggerated. When William
Crimsworth recoils from the flirtatiousness of the "Belgian
beauties" in his classroom, explaining that "we scorn what,
unasked, is lavishly offered," we recognize a not uncommon
human response. The response is, however, a negative one, and
Crimsworth takes a perverse pride in making it. In characters
like Crimsworth, Jane, Frances Henri, or Lucy Snowe this streak
of obstinacy is quiet, perhaps because the dark insurrection this
perverseness bespeaks is kept in check by the conservatism
forced upon them by limited means and low station. In characters like Shirley or Rochester or Mr. Yorke, contumaciousness
is more flagrant—less profound, healthier because less suppressed. Whatever its vagaries, this quality runs through the
ranks of Brontë's characters, contributing to the strange world
the novels create wherein eccentric beings conflict with normal
society, fitting as well as square pegs into round holes. Let us
examine this perverseness more closely.

The preference of Crimsworth, Rochester, M. Paul, and St.
John Rivers for plain, lowly, and unobtrusive mates is one facet
of this perverseness. There is something obstinate, to say the
least, in Crimsworth's horrified reaction to Pelet's suggestion
that one of Crimsworth's rich pupils might make a fine match,
and his instant communion with Frances Henri, that "chétive,
perverse, ill-shriven child"—to evoke Yorke Hunsden's description. The absolute emotional chastity of Paul Emanuel until
won by the less-than-obvious charms of Lucy Snowe is perhaps
unlikelier still. Rochester at least is experienced, and can base
his preference for plainness upon misfortune with beauty; yet
there is something negative too in his enthusiasm for the physically unprepossessing. It is reminiscent of Hamlet's unhealthy
suspicion of the sensual, and Hamlet-like, Rochester revolts
against past sensuality in language that rings changes on the
theme of corruption with true Shakespearean variety: *blot, con-
tamination, pollution, sullied, bilge water, fetid, foul, manure,
infection, blight, plague-house, corrupt, slime, mud* (*JE*, pp.
130–140). All this revulsion for a few pretty *demimondaines*!
In St. John Rivers this negativism reaches a fanatic pitch. The
most terrible (or comic) scene in *Jane Eyre* is not the panic

of the red-room, not the midnight vigil in the upper stories of Thornfield, but the episode in which St. John Rivers places his watch before him on the table and allows himself fifteen minutes to contemplate the beauty of Rosamond Oliver before he locks her out of his heart forever: "I humoured him: the watch ticked on: he breathed fast and low: I stood silent. Amidst this hush the quarter sped; he replaced the watch, laid the picture down, rose, and stood on the hearth" (*JE*, p. 354). Even the very normal Dr. John Bretton is unmoved by the beauties of the *Cleopatra* or the passion of Vashti, and after disillusionment with the forthrightly physical Ginevra Fanshawe, chooses Paulina, who is ethereal rather than beautiful. Among all this preference for the downright inauspicious, Robert Moore's, " 'Bah! I hate ugliness and delight in beauty . . . . I won't have an ugly wife,' " might almost seem to have come from the pen of another novelist—if, that is, the negative were not more conspicuous in the statement than the positive, and if we were not reminded that this most balanced of Brontë men nearly causes Caroline Helstone to die of grief because, until the last chapters, he perversely refuses to admit his affection.

Charlotte Brontë's women exhibit the same penchant for the unattractive. Frances Henri is fascinated by a man with tufts of dun-colored hair protruding over his ears, spectacles, hollow eyes, and sunken cheeks. If Jane is rapt with Rochester's blunt visage upon first acquaintance ("'You examine me, Miss Eyre . . . do you think me handsome?' " " 'No, sir.' "), she finds him even more suitable when he is marred, scarred, and maimed. Shirley prefers Louis to Robert Moore, although " 'nature has not given him features so handsome, or an air so noble as his kinsman' "; and although Caroline is moved to plead, " 'He is not ugly, Shirley . . . he is not ignoble; he is sad . . .' " (*S*, p. 358). In temperament and appearance Rochester is a beau compared with Paul Emanuel. At its best on his fête-day, Emanuel's appearance commands from Lucy a temperate mixture of enthusiasm and honesty:

Not by the vague folds, sinister and conspirator-like, of his soot-

dark paletôt were the outlines of his person obscured; on the
contrary, his figure (such as it was, I don't boast of it) was well
set off by a civilized coat and a silken vest quite pretty to behold. . . . The little man looked well, very well; there was a
clearness of amity in his blue eye, and a glow of good feeling
on his dark complexion, which passed perfectly in the place of
beauty: one really did not care to observe that his nose, though
far from small, was of no particular shape, his cheek thin, his
brow marked and square, his mouth no rosebud: one accepted
him as he was, and felt his presence the reverse of damping
or insignificant. (V, p. 287)

A height of perversity is reached, however, by Mrs. Pryor,
Caroline Helstone's mother, when she explains that she abandoned her daughter in infancy *because* the child was beautiful
and beauty is a sign of the perverse: " 'I let you go as a babe,
because you were pretty, and I feared your loveliness; deeming
it the stamp of perversity. . . . A form so straight and fine, I
argued, must conceal a mind warped and cruel' " (S, pp. 342–
343).

Just as ugliness draws the Brontë heroine irresistibly, so does
an uncertain masculine temperament: Brontë heroines respond
most ardently when they are accorded—not politeness, not
affection—but severity or even cruelty. "I perceived," remarks
Crimsworth, "that in proportion as my manner grew austere
and magisterial, hers [Frances's] became easy and self-possessed
—an odd contradiction, doubtless, to the ordinary effect in
such cases; but so it was" (P, p. 121). Jane is easiest with
Rochester when he is gruff, and during the interim between
his proposal and the wedding day prefers Rochester's grimaces,
pinches, and severe tweaks of the ear—"fierce favors"—to ca-
resses, ardent pressures of the hand, and kisses. Shirley, in such
a rage that "an obstacle cast across [her] path would be split
as with lightening," grows tame as a lamb at Louis Moore's
knee, and soon is reciting penitently to her tutor *Le Cheval
Dompté* as a "punishment-lesson" (S, p. 386). And Lucy asserts
that it is when M. Paul is really unjust, when his sneers have
made her heart ache, that she is moved to feel true stimulation
and aspiration.

Mlle. Reuter flagrantly exhibits the inverted propensities of Frances Henri, Jane, Shirley, and Lucy. Amiable, suave, but cool with Crimsworth when he is cordial to her, she pursues and grovels when he grows cold. As his disdain mounts, her obsession enmeshes her more tightly: " 'Que le dédain lui sied bien! . . . il est beau comme Apollon quand il sourit de son air hautain.' " But it is not only in her sexual tastes that Mlle. Reuter exhibits perversity: Brontë has given us a brilliant portrait of a warped mind:

> . . . as it was her nature to doubt the reality and undervalue the worth of modesty, affection, disinterestedness—to regard these qualities as foibles of character—so it was equally her tendency to consider pride, hardness, selfishness, as proofs of strength. She would trample on the neck of humility, she would kneel at the feet of disdain; she would meet tenderness with secret contempt, *indifference she would woo* with ceaseless assiduities. *Benevolence, devotedness, enthusiasm, were her antipathies; for dissimulation and self-interest she had a preference*—they were real wisdom in her eyes; *moral and physical degradation, mental and bodily inferiority, she regarded with indulgence;* they were foils capable of being turned to good account as set-offs for her own endowments. *To violence, injustice, tyranny, she succumbed*—they were her natural masters . . . . (*P*, p. 113)

My italics call attention to the syntactical inversions in the passage: the form embodies the perverted values of the character described.

Rochester, Crimsworth, Louis Moore, St. John Rivers, Dr. John, and Paul Emanuel have complementary reactions. Rochester is most fervent when Jane is flippant. St. John scorns what he has—Rosamond Oliver's affection—and seeks what is withheld—Jane's allegiance. The more vehemently she refuses him, the more determined his pursuit becomes, until by sheer force he almost overwhelms her openly expressed antipathy. Even Dr. John, who, like Thomas Mann's Hans Hansen, is one of "the fair-haired breed of the steel-blue eyes," does not entirely stand for the pure and the blithe, but discloses the darker side of his nature when he confesses to Lucy that what allures him most in Ginevra Fanshawe is her disdain. Louis Moore's behavior with Shirley is a variant of the same obstinacy. When Shirley is playing the high-handed heiress, Moore is unperturbed and contents himself with pulling Tartar's ears; when Shirley offers her sympathy in his illness, when she proffers him grapes and desires to hand him water, he turns his head aside. We can understand his coolness here, for Shirley seems blithely unaware that the fever parching him is sexual passion, so that Moore taunts her: " 'I do not believe my illness is infectious: I scarcely fear" (with a sort of smile) "you will take it . . .' " (S, p. 377). Yet Moore's behavior conforms to the insistent pattern. Crimsworth and Paul Emanuel, to whom "a knot of blunders is as sweet as a cluster of nuts," exhibit a similar cross-grained obstinacy: they are kind when Frances and Lucy falter in their lessons, and stern whenever they succeed. Brontë's men and women are thus united in a kind of *concordia discors*: a harmony of perversities.

These characters are in a spotlight which illuminates their personalities plainly. Minor characters abound, however, in which a similar contumaciousness holds sway. Edward Crimsworth, William's brother, is a sadist. He hires William as a clerk in his firm—first, in the hope that he will fail miserably; second, because proximity will provide him with opportunity to persecute his brother. When, on the contrary, William Crimsworth not only does his job expertly but refuses to be crushed by his brother's inhuman treatment (stimulated to achievement like Lucy and Frances by harshness), Edward Crimsworth becomes insanely enraged and throws him out—a reaction that is obviously an intensified version of the severity evinced by Emanuel and Crimsworth when Lucy or Frances succeed instead of fail. While we rather like Crimsworth's only friend, Yorke Hunsden, his behavior is scarcely more attractive than Edward Crimsworth's. To William's face he is outrageously rude, delighting to discover the vulnerable facets of his temperament so that he can apply the lash more effectively. Behind the scenes, Hunsden can be magnanimous enough to purchase and present to Crimsworth the portrait of his dead mother; yet the gesture must be negated: he bestows the portrait in such an insulting manner that Crimsworth's joy is immediately checked and he can only return the picture to its case and thrust it aside. Like Edward Crimsworth, Paul Emanuel, and Crimsworth himself, Hunsden can be kind when there is a question of failure. Believing William to have committed a terrible mistake in marrying a lace-mender, an *ouvrière,* Hunsden suddenly softens: ". . . the polite, considerate manner in which he offered me his hand (a thing he had never done before), convinced me that he thought I had made a terrible fool of myself . . ." (*P*, p. 206).

Of similar stamp are three members of the Yorke family (*Shirley*)—Mr. and Mrs. Yorke and Martin. The occasion of the shooting of Robert Moore illustrates well the perverseness of all three. Mr. Yorke by nature is bluff; he masks his partiality for Moore with gruff assurances that he "cares naught about him," that Robert is "nothing akin" to him or his family (S, p. 131). The sight of Robert Moore prone and bleeding on the road, however, fascinates the Yorkshireman:

> The sight of his blood, welling from the treacherously-inflicted wound, made him indeed the son of the Yorkshire gentleman's heart. The spectacle of the sudden event: of the tall, straight shape prostrated in its pride across the road: of the fine southern head laid low in the dust; of that youth in prime flung at once before him pallid, lifeless, helpless—this was the very combination of circumstances to win for the victim Mr. Yorke's liveliest interest. (S, p. 442)

Yorke's saturnine wife is similarly affected by the tragedy: the incident is "quite in her way, and to her taste." Accustomed to throwing fits of hysterics when her children disobey, she is perfectly delighted when Moore is dragged over her threshold half-dead: the sight of blood, the presence of a "half-murdered man in her best bed—set her straight, cheered her spirits, gave her cap the dash of a turban" (S, p. 442). Not incidentally, MacTurk, the surgeon who attends Moore, "abrupt in his best moods; in his worst, savage," manifests the same delight in adversity: his interest in Moore mounts as Moore's condition worsens, and when bandages are tampered with, followed by a great loss of blood, the case picks up for him considerably (S, pp. 444–445). Martin Yorke possesses the same penchant for the cruel. He amuses himself by telling the love-stricken Caroline Helstone that Moore is going to die. When Caroline is too overcome to react, Martin is deprived of the amusement he anticipated: ". . . it was hardly worth while to frighten the girl, if she would not entertain him in return" (S, p. 449). He relents, partly because disappointed, partly because her reaction reminds him too much of the female blackbird he once heard lamenting for the nestlings he had just crushed with a stone. Martin is complex—not by any means a sheer sadist. Yet this element in his character is marked, and it should be remembered that much of his willingness to help Caroline secretly visit Moore stems not from charity, but from the desire to thwart the members of his household.

Equally negative, although along a different bias, is Caroline Helstone's uncle, the Reverend James Helstone. Before the novel opens, Helstone's wife has already died of a slow decline occasioned by his indifference. His neglect is now accorded to his niece, who exists in his household as a lonely, uncomplaining shadow. Making his neglect all the more heartless is the clergyman's affable gallantry toward any female not of his household. This gallantry does not, however, signal admiration. Quite the reverse: he is charming in proportion to his contempt; hating women, he cannot abide one of the sex unless she is a fool: "So very credulous and frivolous was [Hannah]; so very silly did she become when beseiged with attention, flattered and admired to the proper degree, that there were moments when Helstone actually felt tempted to commit matrimony a second time . . ." (S, p. 91). It is unfortunate, incidentally, that lack of a coherent point of view makes Shirley a failure as a work of art, for minor characters like the Yorkes and Helstone are far more psychologically subtle than the rather obvious Mrs. Reed and Mrs. Fairfax, who succeed better, however, because of the structural excellence of Jane Eyre.

To these portraits of the perverse can be added the unholy

league of Miss Scatcherd and Helen Burns, the mother-child relationship of Mme. Beck and her children, and the unlikely association of Lucy Snowe and Ginevra Fanshawe. Like Brontë's "masters," Miss Scatcherd is relatively lenient with her mediocre pupils but harsh with her best. This harshness, of course, goes far beyond Emanuel or Crimsworth's, for in the light of modern psychology Miss Scatcherd is obviously a sadistic lesbian who both masks and indulges her attraction to Burns in the physical chastisements she forces her to undergo. Burns's unnatural submission to cruelty is presented as Christian stoicism; rather, however, it is a complementary response to Miss Scatcherd's sadism, and we must conclude that when Burns docilely fetches the bundle of twigs and readily bares her neck for the whipping, both are more in their element than out of it. Mme. Beck is still another character who is rather delighted than dismayed by pain. Always cool with her children, she is at her best when Fifine is shrieking with the pain of a broken arm. Lucy calls it stoicism, Dr. John "a *sang-froid bien opportun,*" but the reader is apt to conclude that Mme. Beck's icy calm is more frightening than admirable. The association of Lucy Snowe and Ginevra Fanshawe is founded on antipathies: of all types, Ginevra is the kind of frivolous, vain, pretty, selfish creature Lucy cannot abide; of all creatures, Lucy is the kind of obscure, plain, sour personality Ginevra most despises. Yet Ginevra is drawn to Lucy's room like a magnet to hear her character reviled by the sharp and sour Lucy; in the refectory she seeks Lucy's side so that she can dig her elbows into Lucy's ribs and draw down upon her head Lucy's temper. And while Lucy protests that Ginevra's company only irritates her, her ardent love-making in man's guise to this same detested Miss Fanshawe and Ginevra's equally ardent response reveal the hidden currents of this antifriendship. Lucy claims the overacting to be inspired by the desire to taunt Doctor John; we are more apt to join with Paul Emanual, however: "Between the acts M. Paul told us he knew not what possessed us . . ."!

It should be emphasized again that these characters are not at all unlikely: in their perverseness lies much of their realism and complexity. We must remember too that harshness, blunt manners, a tendency to be cool or even surly unless there is good cause for charity is characteristic of Yorkshire and Northern peoples in general. Refined Londoners expressed shock and disbelief at the coarseness of even the gentry in Charlotte Brontë's novels, claiming that people of birth do not behave with such crudity.[15] Rather than accept the verdict of the outsider, however, we should give credence to the opinion of Brontë's local readers who found her characters—even the blatant Blanche Ingram—true to life. Yet the unusual prevalence in both major and minor characters of a rebelliousness, a stubbornness, a certain crabbed obstinacy, a compulsion to be negative or perverse, combined with the reflection of these traits in the style of the novels signals this to be more than just a case of environmental realism: this fascination with the perverse must lie deep-embedded in the personality of the writer herself.

III

In the light of what has been discovered so far, another stylistic trait takes on interest because it tallies so neatly with the perverseness that Brontë's syntactical inversions expose. Charlotte Brontë's pages are heavy with negatives. Without too much exaggeration, one can say that she is as disposed to describe things in terms of what they *are not*, as in terms of what they *are*. Occasionally this negativism is functional and—for the alert reader—keenly effective. It is artistically appropriate, for example, that the perversely heartless Mme. Beck should

15. Brontë neatly retaliates against this criticism in her next novel (*Shirley*). On one occasion, the detestable Donne remarks: " 'Wretched place—this Yorkshire . . . . I could never have formed an idea of the country had I not seen it; and the people—rich and poor—what a set! How corse and uncultivated! They would be scouted in the south.' . . . you must excuse Mr. Donne's pronunciation, reader," explains the narrator, "it was very choice; he considered it genteel, and prided himself on his southern accent; northern ears received with singular sensations his utterance of certain words . . ." (p. 226).

be described largely in negatives: there is something sinister in Lucy's statements that "there *never* was a mistress whose rule was milder," or that Mme. Beck was *never* seen to remonstrate (see especially V, pp. 61–63). The foreshadowing of the thwarted wedding by the negative cast given to the sentences describing Jane Eyre's anticipation is another case in point:

> There was *no* putting off the day that advanced . . . . I, at least, had *nothing* more to do: there were my trunks . . . tomorrow, at this time, they would be far on their road to London: and so should I . . . or rather, *not* I, but one Jane Rochester, a person whom as yet I knew *not*. The cards of address alone remained to nail on . . . I could *not* persuade myself to affix them . . . . Mrs. Rochester! She did *not* exist: she would *not* be born till to-morrow . . . *not* to me appertained that suit of wedding raiment . . . . It was *not* only the hurry of preparation that made me feverish; *not* only an anticipation of the great change . . . . I had at heart a strange and anxious thought. Something had happened which I could *not* comprehend; *no one* knew of or had seen the event but myself . . . .
> (*JE*, p. 261)

It will be remembered that Jane then seeks to cool her fevered anxiety in the garden of Thornfield. There she sees the riven chestnut tree which is also described in terms of what it is not: although the cloven halves are *not* broken from each other, the sap can flow *no more*; it will *never* have green leaves *more*, *never more* see birds making nests in its branches; yet, although its time of pleasure is *over*, the tree is *not* desolate (*JE*, p. 262). The negative adverb, expressing at once impending tragedy and faint hope, is thus used here with striking effect.

On the other hand, the motives for describing a heroine as vivid as Shirley Keeldar in negatives are less clear. We are told that she has *no* Christian name, that she is *no* ugly heiress; that her height and shape are *not* unlike Caroline's, she is *not* a blond like Caroline, her eyes have *no* green lights in them, her features are *not* high, bony, and Roman, and their expressiveness is "*not* to be understood, *nor* their language interpreted all at once" (S, p. 158). Puzzling, too, are the many descriptions of nature in which we are told what the scenery, the view, or the weather is *not* like:

> This night is *not* calm: the equinox still struggles in its storms. The wild rains of the day are abated: the great single cloud disparts and rolls away from heaven, *not* passing and leaving a sea all sapphire, but tossed buoyant before a con- tinued . . . tempest. . . . *No* Endymion will watch for his god- dess to-night: there are *no* flocks out on the mountains; and it is well, for to-night she welcomes Æolus. (S, p. 408)

While a certain Miltonic or Wordsworthian impressiveness is created by these negatives, the reader is also put to task. The night is not calm? It must then be stormy: this is confirmed. A "sea all sapphire" is fine description, but then it appears that, on the contrary, this is what the sea does not look at all like. And, as a final effort, we must depopulate the earth of both Endymion and his flocks.

This insistent negativism has several explanations, one of which has been offered by Karl Kroeber, who states: "Charlotte Brontë gives physical descriptions to her characters because she conceives of them as existing, to a considerable degree, only through their antagonism to others and their resistance to external circumstances."[16] This conception of character ac- counts for the description, as Kroeber suggests, of Mr. Yorke as "inelegant," "unclassic," "unaristocratic," and "indocile"; it also accounts, I believe, for Brontë's warning to her readers that Shirley is unlike the conventional heiress who has a Chris- tian name and is likely to be ugly; it accounts for her insistence that although Rochester may appear a Byronic hero, his blunt manner and his craggy features prevent him from fitting the conventional mold. For Brontë is aware not only that her char- acters bear little resemblance to the real-life acquaintances of her readers, but also that her "chétive, perverse, ill-shriven" creations violate the fictional types that her readers have been accustomed to meet in the pages of the novel. This awareness

---

16. Karl Kroeber, *Styles in Fictional Structure* (Princeton, 1971), p. 29.

of the difference of her fiction extends to plot, theme, and action as well. The "dear reader" device is characteristic, of course, of nineteenth-century fiction in general; it is significant, however, that virtually all Brontë's addresses to her readers admonish that here is matter foreign to common experience or opinion, although realistic and true in the deepest sense nevertheless. "Say what you will, reader—" cries Lucy Snowe, "tell me I was nervous, or mad; affirm that I was unsettled by the excitement of that letter; declare that I dreamed; this I vow—I saw there—in that room—on that night—an image like—a NUN" (V, p. 210). Or, more seriously, Brontë's narrator will advise the reader that her point of view differs and will continue to differ from that of the majority: "I am aware, reader, and you need not remind me, that it is a dreadful thing for a parson to be warlike: I am aware that he should be a man of peace . . . yet . . . you need not expect me to join in your deep anathemas, at once so narrow and so sweeping . . . in horror and denunciation of the diabolical rector of Briarfield" (S, p. 27). There is a continual tension in Brontë's novels arising from her consciousness of her public and her consciousness that what she is writing is often alien to its sympathies.

The fact that the negativism is so prevalent, present not only in character description, but conspicuous in narrative and dialogue as well, indicates, however, that it is for Brontë a natural rather than a deliberate mode of expression, a stylistic indication of her view of reality. Just as her characters are atypical, defined by the expectations they violate rather than fulfill, so their experiences are atypical, characterized by deprivation rather than fulfillment: Shirley Keeldar is Brontë's one attempt at imagining a personality shaped by fortuitous experience. It is necessary, then, that characters whose expectations are so humble, whose opportunities are so limited, whose lives are so obscure (judged, at least, by society's standards) should express themselves and be expressed in negative and pessimistic rather than positive terms. The Brontë protagonist is seldom joyful, for example; rather she is described as *not unhappy*. Veiled in a similar dubiousness are the many half-negative statements such as the description of the food at Lowood as reviving vitality if not satisfying hunger, or Jane's plea that if she not be granted liberty, then at least a new servitude which must be right "because it does not sound too sweet"; Bessie's appraisal of the grown-up Jane "which though it expressed regard, did in no shape denote admiration," or Jane's remark that she does not like Mrs. Fairfax the worse for being a dependent; the description of Louis Moore musing "not unblissfully" against the mantel; Lucy's statement, "Experience lay before me on no narrow scale," or her whole description of Monsieur on his fête-day which ends with the remark that Paul Emanuel's good humor made his pupils feel his presence "the reverse of damping or insignificant." Examples could be compounded almost endlessly.

This insistent negativism adds to the against-the-grain impact of the frequently inverted word order, and at the same time, reinforces the perverse quality of the characters' personalities—and the personality of their creator. Negativism is closely allied to another quality strongly marked in both the author and her novels, however, for negatives are also the trademark of the moralist and the love of "moral kicking" is characteristic not only of Charlotte Brontë, but of her age. While the teachings of Jesus are notably positive, Old Testament law is heavily repressive: one does not need to go further than the Ten Commandments for evidence of this fact: thou shalt *not*. In her dissentient approach to Christian morality Charlotte Brontë shows a marked affinity with the spirit of Mosaic law, a spirit quite opposed to the Christian humanism of George Eliot, for example. This affinity, coupled with an ardent though heavy-handed sincerity, seldom allows her to let her reader deduce the negative from the positive statement for himself. Right must be persistently presented in terms of wrong.

Thus didacticism seems the best explanation for the otherwise incomprehensible negativism of that curious *devoir* of Shirley's which Louis Moore recites from memory: the mating of Eva (Humanity) with a son of God (Genius). The setting is a primitive wilderness; the "human nursling" Eva:

There is something in the air of this clime which fosters life

kindly . . . . Its gentle seasons exaggerate *no* passion, *no* sense
. . . . *Not* grotesquely fantastic are the forms of cliff and foilage;
not violently vivid the colouring of flower and bird . . . . The
gentle charm vouchsafed to flower and tree,—bestowed on deer
and dove,—has *not* been denied to the human nursling. . . .
Nature cast her features in a fine mould; they have matured in
their pure, accurate first lines, *un*altered by the shocks of dis-
ease. *No* fierce dry blast has dealt rudely with the surface of her
frame; *no* burning sun has crisped or withered her tresses: her
form gleams ivory-white through the trees; her hair flows
plenteous, long, and glossy; her eyes, *not* dazzled by vertical
fires, beam in the shade large and open, and full and dewy . . . .
You see in the desolate young savage *nothing* vicious or vacant;
she haunts the wood harmless and thoughtful . . . . (S, pp. 381–
382)

Escapism? Rousseauistic nature worship? Hardly. What at first
looks like flamboyant romanticizing becomes at second glance
flamboyant racism—a firm statement of that most benighted
of Victorian creeds, white supremacy. For what Eva, the savage
nursling, is not, the primitive peoples of the world, according
to Charlotte Brontë, are: passionate, sensual, grotesquely fantastic, violently vivid, grossly moulded, diseased, black, crisped
and withered, narrow and dull-eyed, vicious, vacant, harmful,
and incapable of thought. Charlotte Brontë, who could present
that tool of British imperialism in India, St. John Rivers, as a
great man of God, displays here one of the ugliest aspects of
Victorianism with a naiveté which might be amusing if it were
not at the same time unfortunately ignorant. One would think
Tennyson's *Locksley Hall* lay open before her when she composed that passage:

> I, to herd with narrow foreheads, vacant of
>   our glorious gains,
> Like a beast with lower pleasures, like a beast
>   with lower pains!
> Mated with a squalid savage—what to me
>   were sun or clime?
> I the heir of all the ages, in the foremost files
>   of time—

Is it inconsistent that the negativism, identified with a perverse, rebellious grain in Charlotte Brontë's nature, should also bespeak the moralist? Quite the reverse, for who can admonish and restrict better than one who knows cause? It is perhaps inconsistent that the author's trick of syntactical inversion should lend the novels at once their poetry and their perverseness, but then the tension of inconsistencies is precisely the quality that defines Charlotte Brontë's fiction best.

3

ANTITHESIS

STRUCTURE, ACTION, SETTING, AND CHARACTER

"My Robert! I wish I could justly call him mine: but I am poverty and incapacity; Shirley is wealth and power . . . . This is no sordid suit: she loves him—not with inferior feelings: she loves, or WILL love, as he must feel proud to be loved. . . . As for being his sister, and all that stuff, I despise it. I will either be all or nothing to a man like Robert . . . . Once let that pair be united, and I will certainly leave them. As for lingering about, playing the hypocrite, and pretending to calm senti- ments of friendship, when my soul will be wrung with other feelings, I shall not descend to such degradation. As little could I fill the place of their mutual friend as that of their deadly foe: as little could I stand between them as trample over them. Robert is a first-rate man—in my eyes: I HAVE loved, DO love, and MUST love him. I would be his wife, if I could; as I cannot, I must go where I shall never see him. There is but one alterna- tive—to cleave to him as if I were a part of him, or to be sun- dered from him wide as the two poles of a sphere. Sunder me then, Providence. (S, p. 204)

Evident in this passage from Shirley are two other highly characteristic qualities of Charlotte Brontë's prose style: a language of feeling that is reined in by structures based upon contrasts between antitheses. Of the language, more later; let us consider first Brontë's use of antithesis—briefly as syntactic structure, in more detail as a vehicle through which major motifs are established, which in turn provide a thematic basis of organization for the four novels.

This antithetical balancing operates on four levels which are distinct yet simultaneous, related by a process perhaps best described as a foliation from structure into theme. On the first level, contrast is a way of ordering individual sentences. No less than twelve major antitheses discipline the highly emotional content of the passage from *Shirley* quoted above: (1) poverty and incapacity / wealth and power; (2) (not) inferior feelings / (but) as he must feel proud to be loved; (3) loves / *will* love; (4) all / nothing; (5) united / leave; (6) pretending to calm sentiments / other feelings; (7) mutual friend / deadly foe; (8) stand between / trample over; (9) *have* loved / *do* love; (10) could / cannot; (11) to cleave / to be sundered; (12) she loves or *will* love / I *have* loved, *do* love. Four of these antitheses depend for their effect simply upon semantic contrast. The other eight, however, involve parallel grammatical structures as well: I am / Shirley is; if I could / as I cannot; to cleave / to be sundered, and so forth. The total effect of the passage, therefore, conveys thought as well as feeling, emotion controlled as well as expressed.

Constructions like these are frequent in the novels, giving to Brontë's prose the sense of judicious weighing and epigrammatic thrust. These are achieved, for example, in the description of Georgiana and Eliza Reed by the juxtaposition of *acrid* with *savourless, judgment* with *feeling,* and *draught* with *morsel:* "True, generous feeling is made small account of by some; but here were two natures rendered, the one intolerably acrid, the other despicably savourless for the want of it. Feeling without judgment is a washy draught indeed; but judgment untempered by feeling is too bitter and husky a morsel for human deglutition" (*JE*, pp. 224–225).

Beyond the confines of the sentence, on a second level, this sort of antithesis can structure a chapter or chapters, or—more loosely—the shape of an entire novel. To pursue the example

of Brontë's delineating the natures of Georgiana and Eliza Reed
by antithesis, we find that the contrasting characters of the two
sisters serve to organize chapter 21 of *Jane Eyre*: Georgiana
and Eliza's different appearance, their dissimilar behavior to
Jane, the contrast of their daily occupations—one ceaselessly
active to no purpose, the other totally indolent, their final quar-
rel over irreconcilable predilections for asceticism and luxury—
all these provide a background for Jane that is at once pat-
terned and dramatically conflicting. Coming as it does virtually
at the dead center of the novel, the chapter structurally focuses
the choice Jane will be forced to make upon her return to
Thornfield: shall she lead the luxurious and idle life of Rochester's mistress, or, denying him altogether, force herself to accept
the uncongenial state of an ascetic and morbid chastity. The
necessity of synthesizing two extremes—perhaps the main
theme of the novel—is here established through formal means
alone.

Similarly, Caroline Helstone's contrast of Shirley's wealth
and power with her own poverty and incapacity involves more
than a neatly antithetical locution. The contrast between Shirley and Caroline's social and private lives forms the structure
of several chapters which alternately describe one girl's life and
then the other's. This juxtaposition occurs most patently in the
chapter "Two Lives": Shirley's profitable activity, careless good
nature, and luxurious indolence constitute the first half of the
chapter, while the second half depicts in contrasting paragraphs
which expand the original antithesis, the existence of Caroline
—solitary, morbid, and purposeless. Again, the structure of the
part formally embodies the theme of the whole: more broadly,
the antithesis between poverty and wealth can be advanced
as the chief topic of *Shirley*, for throughout the novel the poor
and the rich continually clash, from the private antagonisms of
Louis Moore and his employers to the epic struggles of the la-
boring against the managerial class.

On the level of the entire novel, antithesis quite clearly provides the basis of structure for *Jane Eyre*. The novel is divided
into five parts chiefly by location: Gateshead, Lowood, Thornfield, Moor House and Morton, and Ferndean. Unification is
provided by the fact that these linear segments are combined

paradigmatically through contrast. In part one, Gateshead, Jane Eyre's position is the opposite of her position in part five: at Gateshead she is an outsider, despised and penniless, rejected by the Reed family; at Ferndean she has banished all outsiders and has triumphed over her humble beginnings as the wife of Rochester and the mistress of the manor. Part four, the Moor House-Morton section, reverses the situation of part two, Lowood. At Lowood Jane is a charity student, browbeaten by the minister Brocklehurst, and befriended in her misery by the sympathetic Miss Temple and Helen Burns. In the fourth segment, the same cast of characters appears, slightly metamorphosized: Mary and Diana Rivers now offer Jane sympathy rather than Miss Temple and Helen Burns, and Brocklehurst reappears in a nobler, though no less fanatic guise, as St. John Rivers. Although St. John bullies and interrogates like Brocklehurst, the situations are antithetical: Jane in part four is a teacher rather than a dependent student, and far from being accused of wickedness, is recognized as a potentially courageous and devoted soldier of God by Rivers. Part three, Thornfield, the longest segment of the novel and its apex, can itself be analyzed as consisting of two contrasting parts: Jane's sojourn there as governess, and, after Rochester's declaration of love, the remainder of her stay as his betrothed. The division of part three also serves as a division of the whole novel into two major, contrasting halves: Jane as an essentially friendless dependent and Jane as an independent teacher and legatee, beloved by Rochester.

Perhaps the most dramatic instance of structure based upon antithesis occurs in *Villette*. One of the most striking and persistent motifs of the novel is the theme of privation and plenty, a theme that is often expressed in balanced antitheses of hunger and nourishment, of thirst and thirst quenched. Here, for example, is Lucy speaking of Dr. John: "'He may write once. . . . But it CANNOT be continued—it MAY not be repeated. Great were that folly which should build on such a promise—insane that credulity which should mistake the transitory rain-pool, holding in its hollow one draught, for the perennial spring yielding the supply of seasons'" (V, p. 196). Far from a casual metaphor, the fluctuation of Lucy Snowe's existence between

emotional starvation and gratification, between have and have-
not, provides the basic structural pattern of the novel. Gratification is no sooner granted than it is tempered or withdrawn,
and thus Lucy's life proceeds, almost chapter by chapter, torn
back and forth between the two extremes of emotional poverty
and wealth. A brief résumé will illustrate the pattern. *Villette*
opens with Lucy happy among her friends at Bretton, but the
halcyon days end abruptly, and we are told, in metaphor of
storm and wreck that tragedy befalls Lucy's family: "The ship
was lost, the crew perished" (*V*, p. 30). Shortly after, a position
offering security and a rather dubious satisfaction falls in Lucy's
way, but is terminated abruptly by the death of her employer,
Miss Marchmont, and once again Lucy Snowe is cast adrift.
Madame Beck's *pensionnat* offers a more permanent security,
but does not guarantee the heroine a tranquil or a satisfying
life. Lucy's success as a teacher, her rise in Madame's establishment, culminating in her personal triumph as an actress on the
eve of Madame's fête, gives way to her severest emotional crisis:
the mental depression brought on by the solitude of the long
vacation. At lowest ebb, happiness flows back again: awakening
from a physical and mental collapse, Lucy finds herself magi-
cally restored to friends, goodwill, and comfort; yet the visit at
La Terrasse must end, and Lucy returns to the *pensionnat*, solitude, and "the palsy of custom." But Dr. John sends the prom-
ised letter, the "taste of fruition"; Lucy's ties with the outer
world are not snapped, and she ventures to formulate a new
creed—a belief in happiness. Utter happiness is then followed
by utter misery: "seven weeks as bare as seven sheets of blank
paper." She is once more rescued from emotional starvation by
Mrs. Bretton's letter and by the formation of ties with the de
Bassompierres; this new friendship, however, only serves to
sever an old one, and the burial of the precious letters from Dr.
John and all her hopes of him follows.

From its beginning, the relationship of M. Paul and Lucy also
follows the pattern of privation and plenty—or rather, of amity
and discord, but this does not seriously affect Lucy's state of
mind until their regard is openly expressed. From that point
the pattern of amity alternating with estrangement can be
traced with ease. M. Paul's confession of friendship on the oc-

casion of the country breakfast is followed by Lucy's errand to the Rue des Mages and Père Silas's warning that close ties with Paul Emanuel are impossible. The new warmth of their relationship, the subject of the chapter "Fraternity," turns cold as the result of priestly interference in the very next chapter, "The Apple of Discord." "Sunshine"—Lucy's final acceptance and blessing of Graham and Paulina's love—is followed by "Cloud": the frustration (as Lucy believes) by Madame Beck and Père Silas of all her hopes, the imminent departure of M. Paul, the harrowing and nightmarish fête—a series of disasters which culminates in Lucy's despairing cry: "My heart will break!" The novel ends in balance with the granting of one heart's desire and the withholding of another: Lucy gains the school in the Faubourg Clothilde, but loses Paul Emanuel, and the novel draws to a close with the paradox of the returning sun whose "light was night to some." We know, of course, that Charlotte Brontë deliberately altered the ending of *Villette* from tragedy to ambiguity to please her father. While the alteration creates some sort of ultimate tension between have and have-not, the pattern of fulfillment and denial which forms the basic structure of the novel demands the death of Paul Emanuel. What is given must in some measure be taken away, for, unlike Graham and Paulina, Lucy is not a favorite child of Fate.

A paradigm makes the structure of *Villette* clear:

Chap.	Plenty	Chap.	Privation
1–3	Bretton	4	"shipwreck"
4	Miss Marchmont	5–7	Lucy adrift
8–14	success as teacher	15	long vacation
16–20	La Terrasse	21	return to Beck's
21–23	letter, theater	24	"seven bare weeks"
24–25	de Bassompierres	26	"A Burial"
33	M. Paul's breakfast	34	Rue des Mages
35	"Fraternity"	36	"Apple of Discord"
37	"Sunshine"	38–39	"Cloud," fête
41	Fauborg Clothilde	42	M. Paul's death

A comparison of Charlotte Brontë's use of antithesis in *The Professor* with its use in *Villette* indicates how far one facet of her technique has developed. *The Professor*, while having its dramatic moments, is little more than the framework of a novel. A large part of the work consists of the barebones of Brontë opinion and idea, unfleshed by incident or action. Much of this statement is cast in balanced antitheses, giving *The Professor* a terse, epigrammatic tone that vastly differs from the fuller, plangent rhythms of *Villette*. The conflict between sensual and rational which Crimsworth *talks* about a great deal in soliloquy foliates into dramatic incident in the later novel: the contrasting claims are dramatized in the subplot of Dr. John-Ginevra-Paulina; in Lucy's experiences with the *Cleopatra* and Vashti; in the ironic contrast between M. Paul and the household he supports in the Rue des Mages; in the conflict between Père Silas, Catholic, and Lucy Snowe, Protestant; and above all, within Lucy herself in a struggle that centers about Dr. John, M. Paul, and that symbolic figure—the nun. Compared with this richness, *The Professor* is barren ground indeed. Charlotte Brontë's preface to her first novel has been called disingenuous on the grounds that the novel does not deny emotion as the preface claims.[1] The preface does not really deny emotion, however; rather it eschews literary romance and sensationalism for the "plain and homely." While much of this plain and homely centers in the characters who must work their way through life, the plainness of *The Professor* arises equally from its style; that is, from the trenchant antithetical statement that characterizes so much of the narrative, which in turn comprises the bulk of the novel.

II

We can identify still a third level of structure as comprising the formal means of creating action, setting, time, and charac-

1. Robert Martin, *The Accents of Persuasion* (London, 1966), p. 26.

terization. On this level, Brontë uses antithesis frequently to dramatize and shape moments of action that are particularly significant to plot and theme. Such a moment occurs, for example, when Lucy Snowe makes the momentous decision to become a teacher rather than remain a *gouvernante*-nurse to Madame Beck's children; when, in other words, she decides to relinquish privacy for an active social role. The episode (V, pp. 65–66) is formed by a series of conflicts between opposing choices. Describing the limited life which Madame Beck now asks her to cast off, Lucy defines its duality: ". . . I seemed to hold two lives—the life of thought, and that of reality; and, provided the former was nourished with a sufficiency of the strange necromantic joys of fancy, the privileges of the latter might remain limited to daily bread, hourly work, and a roof of shelter" (V, p. 65). Lucy chooses reality, a decision forged in the clash of opposing wills: the dominating, stern, masculine nature of Madame Beck rouses the passive yet stubborn Lucy through the same kind of catalytic magic exhibited later by M. Paul; in Lucy's words, "It seemed as if a challenge of strength between opposing gifts was given"—*her* kind of power versus *my* kind of power. The wording of Madame Beck's challenge is also couched in an antithesis at once literal and symbolic: " 'Will you,' " Madame says, " 'go backward or forward?' indicating with her hand, first, the small door of communication with the dwelling-house, and then the great double portals of the classes or school-rooms." *Thought, small door, backward* are rejected, at least for the moment; Lucy goes forward, through the great double portals, to reality.

Similarly, the reader's (and Jane Eyre's) introduction to Rochester is skillfully created from the antithetical clash of the imagined with the actual. Alone after sunset in an unfrequented lane, Jane hears the hoofbeats of an approaching horse:

> As this horse approached, and as I watched for it to appear through the dusk, I remembered certain of Bessie's tales, wherein figured a North-of-England spirit, called a "Gytrash"; which, in the form of horse, mule, or large dog, haunted solitary ways,

and sometimes came upon belated travellers, as this horse was now coming upon me. . . . I heard a rush under the hedge, and close down by the hazel stems glided a great dog, whose black and white colour made him a distinct object against the trees. It was exactly one mask of Bessie's Gytrash,—a lion-like creature with long hair and a huge head . . . . (*JE*, p. 108)

Jane and the reader are swept into the realm of the mysterious. What follows, however, is the antithesis of mystery and snaps the spell abruptly: "The horse followed,—a tall steed, and on its back a rider. The man, the human being, broke the spell at once . . . goblins, to my notions . . . could scarce covet shelter in the common-place human form. No Gytrash was this,—only a traveller taking the short cut to Millcote" (*JE*, p. 108). Metaphor likens two ostensibly dissimilar entites by yoking them together, antithesis differentiates between two entities by the same method: the bluntness, the solidity, the no-nonsense vitality of Rochester is established immediately by setting him in relief against an atmosphere of mystery and fairy tale. Yet, once suggested, the romantic half of the antithesis is never quite abolished; it remains as an unfulfilled possibility in the reader's mind, giving another dimension to Rochester's personality—despite the disclaimer.

Examples, of course, can be compounded. In *The Professor*, Crimsworth, after a long search for Frances Henri, finds her and asks her to marry him in a scene that can be considered the emotional apex of the novel. After this idyllic episode by the fire, Crimsworth returns to his lodging. Sleepless, he lies in bed in a "sweet delirium" and "troubled ecstasy." Suddenly he hears a voice saying: "In the midst of life we are in death":

A horror of great darkness fell upon me; I felt my chamber invaded by one I had known formerly, but had thought forever departed. I was temporarily a prey to hypochondria.

She had been my acquaintance, nay, my guest, once before in boyhood . . . . No wonder her spells THEN had power; but NOW, when my course was widening, my prospect brightening; when my affections had found a rest; when my desires, folding wings, weary with long flight, had just alighted on the very

lap of fruition, and nestled there warm, content, under the
caress of a soft hand—why did hypochondria accost me now?
I repulsed her as one would a dreaded and ghastly concubine
coming to embitter a husband's heart toward his young bride
.... (*P*, pp. 202–203)

That Brontë is using antithesis quite consciously to structure
this segment of the novel is proved by the amusingly naïve and
blunt address to the reader in which she plainly reveals the
scaffolding behind the stage set: "Now, reader, during the last
two pages I have been giving you honey fresh from flowers,
but you must not live entirely on food so luscious; taste then a
little gall—just a drop, by way of change" (p. 201). Brontë is
undoubtedly unaware, however, of the subtle ambivalences this
dramatic contrast between joy and horror reveals. While in one
sense a "reaction" after feeling intense joy is a common phenomenon, the violence of Crimsworth's attack (it is a fortnight
until he is well) betrays the depths of his mental agitation.
When we examine the antitheses established in this bit of action (pp. 201–203) we find: life / death; sweet delirium, ecstasy / horror of darkness; sky, sun, grass, and green tree / death
cold bosom, arms of bone, black sullen river; many affections /
few objects; glowing aspirations / gloomy prospects; strong
desires / slender hopes; lap of fruition / vaulted home of horrors; young bride / dreaded and ghastly concubine. Brontë
explains this attack of hypochondria as an intense fear of death
following immediately upon Crimsworth's belief in a new life
with Frances, and we can allow the psychological probability
of this reaction. It is interesting to note, however, how closely
this new life is identified in Crimsworth's mind with passion or
sexuality as the words *delirium, ecstasy, glowing, strong desires,* and *lap of fruition* indicate. The language suggests (if
Brontë does not) that Crimsworth's mental depression is a
reaction in part against the sexuality, the "fruition" that marriage promises; a subconscious revulsion against the very relationship he has desired for so long. Predictably, he thus repulses
the symbol of sexual experience, the dreaded and ghastly concubine, which, in his own words, is in danger of embittering his
heart toward his young bride.

As a final example, one can note how Brontë uses antithesis to structure the scene in *Villette* in which Lucy opens the long-hoped for letter from Dr. John:

> . . . I took my letter, trembling with sweet impatience; I broke its seal.
>
> "Will it be long—will it be short?" thought I, passing my hand across my eyes to dissipate the silvery dimness of a suave, south wind shower.
>
> It was long.
>
> "Will it be cool?—will it be kind?"
>
> It was kind.
>
> To my checked, bridled, disciplined expectation, it seemed very kind: to my longing and famished thought it seemed, perhaps, kinder than it was.
>
> So little had I hoped, so much had I feared; there was a fulness of delight in this taste of fruition—such, perhaps, as many a human being passes through life without ever knowing. The poor English teacher in the frosty garret, reading by a dim candle guttering in the wintry air, a letter simply good-natured —nothing more: though that good-nature then seemed to me god-like—was happier than most queens in palaces. . . . But the cordial core of the delight was . . . that it had been poured out not merely to content ME—but to gratify HIMSELF. A gratification he might never more desire, never more seek—an hypothesis in every point of view approaching the certain; but THAT concerned the future. This present moment had no pain, no blot, no want; full, pure, perfect, it deeply blessed me. A passing seraph seemed to have rested beside me, leaned towards my heart, and reposed on its throb a softening, cooling, healing, hallowing wing. Dr. John, you pained me afterwards: forgiven be every ill—freely forgiven—for the sake of that one dear remembered good! (V, pp. 209–210)

In one brief scene Brontë has thus employed more than a dozen elements of contrast: long / short; kind / cool; checked, bridled, disciplined expectation / longing and famished thought; so little / so much; hoped / feared; the poor English teacher in the frosty garret / most queens in palaces; an hypothesis / the certain; the future / the present moment; pain / perfect; blot / pure; want / full; every ill / one good; and so forth. Clearly this technique achieves dramatic suspense: "Will it be long—will it be short?" But effect and intention go deeper than mere rhetorical drama. Antithesis raises here, as in the hypochondria episode in *The Professor*, the spectre of the death's head at the feast: we are ever reminded that happiness for the Brontë protagonist is seldom untempered by mutual pain; that it is only by a rare stroke of good fortune that Lucy experiences for a moment kindness, hope, and "one dear remembered good." This fragment of *Villette*, like many other scenes in the novel, thus duplicates in structure and theme the larger pattern of the novel discussed above, reiterating the motif of much is given, much is taken away.

Brontë's treatment of time has been discussed in chapter 1. It will be noted that the passage from *Villette* above has as its central antithesis the characteristic Brontëan juxtaposition of time *then* with time *now*, although the juxtaposition here is not that simple since there are other contrasting time planes as well. Lucy's hopes and fears during the days before she receives the letter augment the "fulness of delight" of the moment she actually holds it in her hand. Conversely, Lucy's reflection that although Dr. John has written her this once it is a "gratification he might never more desire" in the future momentarily dims some of her joy in the present. With the remark, "but THAT concerned the future," we abruptly shift from narrative present as the older Lucy's voice breaks in, speaking now, at the writing of the narrative, about the past. This past she further dichotomizes into two time levels: the present moment of receiving the letter and afterwards, when Dr. John will disappoint Lucy. We are then returned to the moment of writing when the older Lucy says, "forgiven be every ill," and the complete time span from the moment of Lucy's opening the letter in the past (but narrative present) to the moment of writing about the experience as an older woman is captured in the phrase "that one dear remembered good." The time scheme is thus very complex, but always functions (as it does frequently in the other novels) to contrast states of feeling, so that we are never permitted hope without fear, expectation without disappointment, fulfillment without privation, joy without pain.

If we examine the setting of the "letter scene," we discover that its effectiveness too derives from its contrast to the action it compasses. "The poor English teacher" takes her letter to the *grenier*, described as deep, black, vast, solitary, and ice-cold; she reads by "a dim candle guttering in the wintry air," reposing on "a doddered and mouldy chest of drawers." In total contrast to these bleak and sterile surroundings are Lucy's emotions, described in images of warmth, fruitfulness, and luxury: Lucy's tears are "the silvery dimness of a suave, south wind shower"; she experiences a "fulness of delight in this taste of fruition"; the letter itself is "a bubble—but a sweet bubble—of real honey-dew." Dr. John writes in a "benignant mood, dwelling with sunny satisfaction on . . . the last few halcyon weeks" in language that is "blithe and genial." The antitheses between icy cold and southern warmth, solitude and emotional gratification are truly startling; we find that this contrast of setting and action is yet another structural statement of the novel's theme of privation and plenty. At the same time, the contrast symbolizes the dual nature of Lucy herself—at once cool, reserved, and puritanical; imaginative, passionate, and demanding. The figure of the nun that appears directly after the reading of the letter, although "real," functions, as critics have pointed out, as a symbol for the chaste, negative side of Lucy's nature. Given Lucy's divided personality, it is not surprising that the emotions (expressed in extremely sensuous terms) aroused by Dr. John's letter should be followed by their antithesis: not by coincidence, Lucy drops and loses the letter at the terrifying sight of the very aspect of her personality that the letter a few moments ago had dispelled.

The Professor is not a novel filled with memorable moments, but two of the more effective episodes occur when Crimsworth finds Frances Henri brooding in the cemetery and when he learns the truth about Zoraïde Reuter's attachment to him. In the first, Brontë uses the same contrast of bleak setting and strongly emotional action. The cemetery is characterized by white walls, pale parapets, gloomy and sinister trees, a massive iron cross, a warm, breathless gloom, languid flowers, and listless cypresses. Here, says Crimsworth, "while following with my eyes the track of sorrow on the turf of a graveyard—here was my lost jewel dropped on the tear-fed herbage, nestling in the mossy and mouldy roots of yew-trees"—Frances Henri (p. 148). He greets her, and her face, in contrast to its pallor and to the sterile gloom of the surroundings, flushes in animation and exquisite pleasure: "It was the summer sun flashing out after the heavy summer shower; and what fertilises more rapidly than that beam, burning almost like fire in its ardour" (p. 148). In the Zoraïde Reuter episode Brontë again contraposes setting with action, but reverses them. The setting is idyllic, romantic: "a moonlight night of summer warmth and serenity," a garden, "varied with silvery lustre and deep shade, and all fresh with dew," a perfume exhaling from the closed blossoms of the fruit trees. Leaning from his window, Crimsworth is just conjuring up ideal visions of Zoraïde when murmurs interrupt his reverie and the moonlight reveals Zoraïde strolling arm and arm with his employer, Pelet, deep in discussion of their forthcoming marriage. Rather than obscuring reality, moonlight reveals here "very plainly, very unequivocally" the truth to Crimsworth, and the beautiful night ironically intensifies the baseness of the woman he thought he loved (pp. 92–96).[2] The scene is repeated in the same chapter (12), with alterations, of course, in *Villette*: Lucy wanders solitary in the gardens and *allée défendue* of the *pensionnat* where she is accustomed to go "to keep tryst with the rising moon" or "taste one kiss of the evening breeze." This idyllic but sexual language continues in the description of vines that "gathered their tendrils in a knot of beauty, and hung their clusters in loving profusion about the favoured spot where jasmine and ivy met, and married them," and flowers which no sun could win that "now answered the persuasion of the dew."[3] Lucy's

2. See Robert Heilman's "Charlotte Brontë, Reason, and the Moon," *NCF* 14 (March 1960): 283–302.

3. Brontë frequently invests nature with sexuality, perhaps nowhere so strenuously as in the scene where Eva (humanity) is wedded to a "son of God" (genius): "The Evening flushed full of hope: the Air Panted; the Moon—rising before—ascended large, but her light showed no shape. 'Lean towards me, Eva. Enter my arms; repose thus.' . . . 'Oh, take me! Oh, claim me! This is a god'" (S, pp. 383–384).

animistic love affair with nature is suddenly interrupted by a concrete manifestation of a real affair: a casket containing a *billet-doux* is thrown down into the *allée* from a window above. The peace of the garden is shattered and again Brontë signals her conscious employment of antagonistic elements with Lucy's remark: "Should not such a mood, so sweet, so tranquil, so unwonted, have been the harbinger of good? Alas, no good came of it! Presently the rude Real burst coarsely in—all evil, grovelling, and repellent as she too often is" (*V*, p. 94).[4]

Given the nature of the typical Brontë protagonist, it is hardly coincidental that setting should so often conflict with the psychic or physical action it encompasses. For Brontë's protagonists are in a basic sense out of place. This alienation is partly created by caste, for while her poor but educated characters are allowed access to the circles of the rich or well-born, their poverty prevents them from belonging there as equals. While Jane Eyre and Louis Moore, by marrying Rochester and Shirley respectively, overcome differences in caste, both novels deal more with Jane and Moore's alienation from society than with their successful integration into it: we remember Jane hidden in the corner of Thornfield's elegant drawing room and isolated at Ferndean, or Moore held up to scorn by Shirley's relatives at Fieldhead. In *The Professor* and *Villette* no attempt is made to pretend that Crimsworth or Lucy feel anything but out of place in the homes of the rich—Crimsworth's brother or Lucy's friends, the de Bassompierres. Even if caste did not

---

4. Charlotte Brontë's habit of consciously contrasting the ideal with the real, like so many traits of her mind and style, is very apparent in her juvenile writings. Homesick at boarding school, indulging in her favorite Angrian fantasy, she writes how she sees before her a "swart and sinewy Moor . . . his broad chest heaving wildly"—when suddenly, "while this apparition was before me, the dining-room door opened and Miss W[ooler] came in with a plate of butter in her hand." And, at another occasion: "I felt as if I could have written gloriously. The spirit of all Verdopolis— of all the mountainous North—of all the woodland West—of all the river-watered East, came crowding into my mind. . . . But just then a dolt came up with a lesson . . ." (T. J. Wise and J. A. Symington, eds., *The Miscellaneous and Unpublished Writings of Charlotte and Patrick Branwell Brontë*, vol. 2 [Oxford, 1936–1938], pp. 124, 255–256).

exclude Brontë's characters from society, disposition would, for in their bluntness, independence, honesty, and self-righteousness they are at odds with the easy social hypocrisies practiced by the majority of the bourgeoisie. Thus Jane finds both Gateshead and Lowood anathema to her rebellious spirit; Lucy is forever a stranger in the elegant concert salon or the smooth, Jesuitical atmosphere of indulgent repression in Madame's *pensionnat*; and even at La Terrasse, she recognizes that, kindly and hospitable as Dr. John and his mother may be, she must always be an outsider in that healthy, lively, prosperous home.

As *Villette* is Brontë's most internal novel, a great deal of narrative being given over to Lucy's reaction to events per se, it is appropriate that many settings take color from her impression of them rather than from objective description. Again, these settings are frequently projected as environments hostile to Lucy's feelings, even though (or perhaps one should say, because) they are largely created by them. Such a setting is the dormitory on the eve of the village fête. Lucy, under the influence of a drug, is emotionally overwrought: "Instead of stupor, came excitement. . . . Imagination was roused from her rest, and she came forth impetuous and venturous. . . . excited, from head to foot—what could I do better than dress?" (*V*, pp. 379–380). To Lucy's fevered imagination, the school becomes a jail from which she must escape, her memories the manacled prisoners. So vivid is the impression that she is amazed at the relative ease of her escape:

> The great classe-doors are close shut; they are bolted. . . . The classes seem, to my thought, great dreary jails, buried far back beyond thoroughfares, and for me, filled with spectral and intolerable memories, laid miserable amongst their straw and their manacles. . . . There is no lock on the huge, heavy, porte-cochère . . . it fastens with a sort of spring-bolt . . . . Can I manage it? It yields to my hand, yields with propitious facility. . . . I wonder as I cross the threshold and step on the paved street, wonder at the strange ease with which this prison has been forced. . . . But here I cannot stay; I am still too near old haunts; so close under the dungeon, I can hear the prisoners moan. (*V*, pp. 380–381)

The event that follows, Lucy's hallucinatory wanderings through the city of Villette during the height of the festivities, has again as its basic structure the contrast between Lucy—solitary, neglected, a mere looker-on—and the brilliance, gaiety, excitement, and conviviality of the thronging crowds. Everyone is richly dressed, Lucy is clad in a plain dress and garden bonnet; everyone is among friends, Lucy is alone; everyone is gay, Lucy is in torment. As in a dream, she sees the people who have meant the most to her: Paulina and Dr. John drive by in a carriage, gazing fondly into each other's eyes; before her at the outdoor concert sit Dr. John and Paulina with Mrs. Bretton, a close, happy family group: "Little knew they the rack of pain which had driven Lucy almost into fever, and brought her out, guideless and reckless . . . ." The evening culminates in what seems to Lucy a horrible verification of M. Paul's desertion: she beholds M. Paul and his ward together, apparently in love, surrounded by approving friends and relatives. Little matter that Lucy's interpretation of the scene is false; the fête episode is a remarkable description of solitary unhappiness among happiness that is created almost entirely by opposing the mental state of protagonist against a setting of external action, with the added psychological dimension that it is the mental state of the protagonist which exaggerates her alienation from the scene.

Finally, on this third level of structure, we find that Charlotte Brontë uses antithesis as a formal means of creating character. In the broadest, nonformal sense (as indicated in the previous chapter), all her characters are created from antithesis in that their appearance, behavior, and opinions are at odds with the fictional prototypes expected by the Victorian reader. Within the novels themselves, however, Brontë consciously structures many of her characters from opposing parts. This is so in the case of Rosamond Oliver, whose facile personality Brontë damns with faint praise in a paragraph of rhetorical antitheses: ". . . she was coquettish, but not heartless; exacting, but not worthlessly selfish. She had been indulged from her birth, but was not absolutely spoilt. She was hasty, but good-humoured; vain . . . but not affected . . . she was very charming . . . but she was not profoundly interesting or thoroughly impressive"

(*JE*, p. 349). Blanche Ingram is characterized in the same consciously balanced way: "She was very showy, but she was not
genuine: she had a fine person, many brilliant attainments; but
her mind was poor, her heart barren by nature . . . . She advo-
cated a high tone of sentiment; but she did not know the sensations of sympathy and pity; tenderness and truth were not in
her" (*JE*, p. 176). The character of Yorke Hunsden is a curious
blend of opposing tendencies: "I discerned," says Crimsworth,

> that there would be contrasts between his inward and out-
> ward man; contentions, too; for I suspected his soul had more
> of will and ambition than his body had of fibre and muscle
> . . . his features might have done well on canvas, but indif-
> ferently in marble . . . expression re-cast them at her pleasure
> . . . giving him now the mien of a morose bull, and anon that
> of an arch and mischievous girl; more frequently, the two
> semblances were blent, and a queer, composite countenance
> they made. (*P*, pp. 27–28)

Similarly, the character of Zoraïde Reuter is assessed by Brontë
in a series of antitheses stemming from the central paradox that
this is a woman cruel to those who are kind and kind to those
who are cruel. As she regards modesty, affection, and disinter-
est as worthless, so she admires pride, hardness, and selfishness
as proofs of strength; "she would trample on the neck of hu-
mility, she would kneel at the feet of disdain . . . ."

Zoraïde Reuter evolved into Madame Beck, a more complex
and realistic character because the antagonizing elements of
her nature are not merely stated antithetically, as in the case
of Rosamond Oliver, Blanche Ingram, and Zoraïde Reuter, but
translated into action. Yet from the beginning, Madame's personality is consciously portrayed by Brontë as a conflict between surface and depth, between the woman she seems to be
and the woman she really is. Lucy's understanding of Madame
Beck's character grows until, in a climactic moment, she turns
upon the woman and charges her with the truth: that under
the smooth, serene, peaceful, and decorous surface Madame
Beck presents to the world, she is a passionate, selfish, indul-

gent sensualist. Lucy achieves this understanding, not incidentally, because she and Madame are alike rather than the opposites they seem. Both are hard-working, independent, proud,
strong-willed personalities. Both hide a passionate nature under
a surface: benign serenity in Madame's case; retiring passivity
in Lucy's. It is inevitable that the conflict between these equals
should end, as it does, in a draw.

The reader tends to think of St. John Rivers as a monolithic
character because of the memorable descriptions of him in
terms of "chiseled marble," "cold as a snow-drift," "a Warrior,"
or "a Greek face." In reality, St. John's character is forged from
the conflict between passion and asceticism, self-indulgence
and denial: the extremity of his rigid self-control is a measure
of the extent to which the opposite obsessions claim him. He
is, as he himself states, a cold, hard man, yet this coldness has
been hard-won, as the episode of Rosamond Oliver's portrait
dramatizes. His words to Jane as he gives rein to the sensual
imaginings he usually represses are a nonpareil in Victorian
literature, another instance of Brontë's uncontrolled imagination and naïveté producing the most astonishing scenes. The
insistent tensions created from the juxtaposition of indulgence
against denial, deliciousness against poison, and flesh against
soul hardly need to be pointed out:

> "Fancy me yielding and melting, as I am doing: human love
> rising like a freshly opened fountain in my mind and over-
> flowing with sweet inundation all the field I have so carefully,
> and with such labour prepared—so assiduously sown with the
> seeds of good intentions, of self-denying plans. And now it is
> deluged with a nectarous flood—the young germs swamped—
> delicious poison cankering them: now I see myself stretched
> on an ottoman in the drawing-room at Vale Hall, at my bride
> Rosamond Oliver's feet: she is talking to me with her sweet
> voice . . . smiling at me with these coral lips . . . my heart is
> full of delight—my senses are entranced . . . .
>
> Now . . . that little space was given to delirium and delusion.
> I rested my temples on the breast of temptation, and put my
> neck voluntarily under her yoke of flowers; I tasted her cup.
> The pillow was burning: there is an asp in the garland: the

wine has a bitter taste: her promises are hollow—her offers false . . . . When I colour, and when I shake before Miss Oliver, I do not pity myself. I scorn the weakness. I know it is ignoble; a mere fever of the flesh: not, I declare, the convulsion of the soul. THAT is just as fixed as a rock, firm set in the depths of a restless sea." (*JE*, pp. 354–356)

It is appropriate that the language of sensuality here is blended with the religious—the labored field, the seeds of good intention, the flood, the cup, the asp in the garland (obviously alluding to Satan in the garden of Eden), the wine. It is appropriate because St. John is a clergyman; it is suggestive of the fact that St. John does not finally abolish his passionate nature, but transfers it to the religion he embraces with such an obsessive fervor. Of all the strong characters in Brontë's novels, St. John is the most violent; it is not too much to say that he is, finally, mad. Although his cold fanaticism repels Jane, she (and Brontë) ultimately admires him, judging him a good man who has fought the good fight for his faith. The final paragraph of *Jane Eyre* eulogizing Rivers suggests that, interestingly enough, Brontë has portrayed convincingly the contradictions of this character without really understanding it.

Georgiana and Eliza Reed are not important enough singly to have complex characters. Taken together, however, they exemplify the conflicting claims of passion and restraint that a whole personality—in this case Jane Eyre herself—is beset with: Georgiana is "feeling without judgment," a "despicably savourless nature"; Eliza is "judgment untempered by feeling," a character "intolerably acrid." And Brontë frequently "splits" a character in this schizoid manner, so that in addition to functioning as individuals, each character also exists thematically as half of a dual personality. The most conspicuously antagonistic pair is, of course, Rochester and St. John Rivers, major representatives of the feeling-judgment duality—Rochester, until his conversion, "feeling without judgment"; Rivers, having renounced his need for human affection, "judgment without feeling." Caroline Helstone and Shirley Keeldar are also consciously presented as antithetical: Caroline is "poverty and incapacity"; Shirley is "wealth and power." More profoundly, Shirley is

Brontë's vision of what woman *could* be given economic independence: forthright, unafraid, vigorous, sensual, aggressive, benevolent. Caroline is what the Victorian young woman *is*: stifled, limited, useless, fearful, sensitive, morbid. Kate Millett has noted this phenomenon in her *Sexual Politics*: "Brontë," she says, "keeps breaking people into two parts so we can see their divided and conflicting emotions." She suggests that Graham Bretton is really two people: one, the adored son seen through the eyes of his mother and the child Polly; the other, the selfish, narcissistic, charming egotist that Lucy knows. Lucy and Polly at the beginning of *Villette* are antagonistic aspects of one normal child: Polly, the adoring sister; Lucy, the envious one. Mrs. Bretton and Madame Beck are two facets of the middle-aged Victorian matron. Both are blooming, efficient, and full of sexual vitality that can find no market. Mrs. Bretton subdues her sexual energy in the cloying, jealous adoration of "my son John," while Madame Beck is driven to find a sexual outlet in patrolling the sexual lives of her young boarders and even of her cousin, M. Paul.[5] Robert and Louis Moore are one person split into two, as are Edward and William Crimsworth. Each pair of brothers is almost identical: proud, individualistic, arrogant, and intelligent. Robert Moore and Edward Crimsworth are the financially and socially capable halves of this personality; Louis Moore and William Crimsworth the eccentric, asocial, rebellious halves that are forced to turn to teaching as an outlet for their talents and aggressions. The most amusing and certainly the most literal character-splitting occurs in *Villette*, when it is discovered that the ghostly nun who haunts Lucy Snowe with the spectre of suppressed sexuality is actually the Count de Hamal, robed and veiled, stalking the premises to keep his amorous appointments as the lover of Ginevra Fanshawe!

Finally, Brontë's novels are peopled with split personalities that are not properly "characters" at all, but symbols of the same antagonistic forces that contend in the minds of real characters. The actress Vashti is "present" for the reader only in

5. Kate Millett, *Sexual Politics* (New York, 1971), pp. 140–147.

Lucy's description; yet as a personality who combines in one nature the angelic and demonic, the spiritual and the sensual, she functions as a symbol of Lucy's divided personality, and Lucy's violently ambivalent reaction to the actress's performance is one of the most revealing moments in the novel. Shirley's vividly imagined verbal portrait of Eve—"vast was the heart whence gushed the well-spring of the blood of nations; and grand the undegenerate head where rested the consort-crown of creation"—is another embodiment of the dual qualities of heart and mind. Occasionally real portraits fulfill this function of representing opposing qualities: Jane Eyre paints portraits of both herself and Blanche Ingram and holds them side by side to better remind herself of the disparity between wealth and poverty, beauty and plainness, body and spirit. In *Shirley*, portraits of two brothers hanging side by side exemplify in their contrasting faces principle and steadiness on the one hand, selfishness and unreliability on the other. Lucy Snowe's afternoon in the art gallery finds her confronted by the *Cleopatra*, a gorgeous and over-ripe monument to sensuality and, conversely, a group of drab little pictures depicting the pious life of a good Catholic woman as "Jeune Fille," "Mariée," "Jeune Mère," and "Veuve"—the two ridiculous, mythical extremes Victorian society foisted upon women. Perhaps the most striking symbol in Brontë's fiction of the conflicting claims of body and spirit is Shirley's visionary mermaid, who combines in her fair face and foul, serpentine body the spiritual and the phallic, and, like Vashti, calls forth ambivalent feelings of fascination and abhorence from the protagonist:

> "I am to be walking by myself on deck . . . watching and being watched by a full harvest-moon: something is to rise white on the surface of the sea . . . . I call you [Caroline Helstone] up from the cabin: I show you an image, fair as alabaster, emerging from the dim wave . . . a human face is plainly visible; a face in the style of yours . . . whose straight, pure lineaments paleness does not disfigure . . . it beckons. Were we men, we should spring at the sign . . . being women, we stand safe, though not dreadless. She comprehends our unmoved gaze; she feels herself powerless . . . she cannot charm,

but she will appall us: she rises high, and glides all revealed, on the dark wave-ridge. Temptress-terror! monstrous likeness of ourselves! Are you not glad, Caroline, when at last, and with a wild shriek, she dives?" (S, p.192)

To this vivid recognition that women are, despite vigorous Victorian denial, both spirit and animal, Caroline Helstone and Mrs. Pryor both strenuously object: " 'But Shirley,' " rebukes Caroline, " 'she is not like us: we are neither temptresses, nor terrors, nor monsters.' " Mrs. Pryor, like a prudent Victorian matron, simply sweeps the dust quickly under the rug: " 'We are aware that mermaids do not exist: why speak of them as if they did?' " To which Shirley, that most hermaphrodite of all Brontë's characters, called even, from time to time "the little gentleman," can only reply, " 'I don't know' " (S, p. 193).

III

Many writers use antithesis as a stylistic device, but few critics have ever considered it a characteristic of Charlotte Brontë's prose style. On the contrary, her style has been acknowledged as noteworthy chiefly for its vehemence. To invoke Elizabeth Rigby's review: *Jane Eyre* "bears no impress of being written at all, but is poured out rather in the heat and hurry of an instinct, which flows ungovernably on to its object, indifferent by what means it reaches it, and unconscious too."[6] The presence in Charlotte Brontë's novels of a consciously employed structural framework that shapes not only her prose style, but provides a recurring, organizing principle for plot, setting, character, and action as well should call for pause and reconsideration of epithets like "vehement" and "unconscious."

For we associate the balancing of opposites with the prose styles of Johnson, Gibbon, or Macaulay and with the qualities of deliberation rather than instinct, control rather than ungov-

6. Elizabeth Rigby [Lady Eastlake], *"Vanity Fair—and Jane Eyre," Quarterly Review* 84 (December 1848): 162–176.

ernability, consciousness rather than unconsciousness. Charlotte
Brontë was deeply immersed in the literature of the late eighteenth and early nineteenth centuries, the inheritor (as was all
her age) of the philosophical frame of mind which found a
style of balanced and often antithetical statement congenial.
Her reverence for reason is patent in all her mature writing.
And yet, this reverence, like St. John Rivers's reverence for self-
denial, is created from necessity: it is a measure of how deeply
its opposite quantity—feeling—held a claim on her. Her style,
therefore, despite this trait that we associate with didacticism
and rationality, does not finally impress us as deliberate and
balanced, because other idiosyncracies of her style are not
logical but emotional, and these conflict with her conscious use
of antithetical balance. Besides, Brontë chiefly uses antithesis
to dramatize the conflicting claims upon *one* personality. When
Johnson states that Pope's poetry rises higher but that Dryden's
continues longer on the wing, he is delineating discrete differences between individual writers for purposes of objective comparison. Although the rhetorical method is the same, the effect
is vastly different than the dichotomizing of one personality
into antagonistic forces.

Villette, Shirley, The Professor—even *Jane Eyre*—are not
"novels of passion" even though they contain a great deal of
that quality. Rather they are novels concerned with the dy-
namics of an individual's struggle to balance imagination and
reason, passion and restraint, passivity and aggression in his
nature. Yet, an observation of Harold Martin's has relevance
here; he remarks that Augustan balanced prose is found in the
novels of passion "where balanced clauses serve as restraints
on the otherwise uninhibited excesses of declaration, protest,
ecstasy, grief, and romantic despair."[7] With a great deal of
qualification, this, I believe, can be said to be the effect of
antithesis in Charlotte Brontë's novels. What is not applicable
to Brontë's fiction is the phrase "otherwise uninhibited." In the
first place, as we have seen, the balancing of opposites charac-

7. Harold C. Martin, "The Development of Style in Nineteenth-
Century American Fiction," in *Style in Prose Fiction,* ed. Martin (New
York, 1959), p. 126.

terizes not only Brontë's prose style, but all formal aspects of her fiction. In the second place, the most "passionate" moments in the four novels (*The Professor* boasts hardly any) virtually all deal with the struggle *against* ecstasy, grief, and romantic despair. The passage quoted above from *Shirley* in which Caroline gives up Robert Moore is a case in point. If an uninhibited moment ever occurs in a Brontë novel, it is immediately suppressed: the turbidly sexual dream Jane has of being reunited with Rochester is followed by a statement like a dash of icewater: "By nine o'clock the next morning I was punctually opening the school; tranquil, settled, prepared for the steady duties of the day" (*JE*, p. 348). In no sense, then, can Brontë's use of antithesis be thought of as a kind of external brake, judiciously applied whenever the pace gets too hot and fast. Rather this facet of her style is an expression of how deeply reason, duty, good sense, and judgment claimed her allegiance and how much of her art was dedicated to their services. Because, however, feeling has a more than equal claim, her style necessarily reflects this too; conflict ensues; and it is this conflict which finally gives the tone to Brontë's fiction.

4

THE LANGUAGE
OF ANTITHESIS

While it has been impossible to avoid discussing language when analyzing three of the planes on which antithesis operates in Charlotte Brontë's novels, the fourth or semantic level merits special attention in itself. Antithesis occurs here more complexly, since it operates simultaneously in several different ways.

First, because Brontë's language is richly figurative—lavish with metaphor, allusion, personification, and analogy—it wars with the sentence structure which, with its antitheses, short clauses, and heavy punctuation, can be characterized as disciplined rather than emotive. This conflict between language and structure can readily be observed if we compare a passage of Austen's prose with a passage of Brontë's, for the effect—despite similar sentence structure—is very different:

> Bingley was endeared to Darcy by the easiness, openness, ductility of his temper, though no disposition could offer a greater contrast to his own, and though with his own he never appeared dissatisfied. . . . In understanding Darcy was the superior. Bingley was by no means deficient, but Darcy was clever.

He was at the same time haughty, reserved, and fastidious, and his manners, though well bred, were not inviting. . . . Bingley was sure of being liked wherever he appeared, Darcy was continually giving offence. (*Pride and Prejudice* [Boston, 1956], p. 11)

Love can excuse anything except Meanness; but Meanness kills Love, cripples even Natural Affection; without Esteem, True Love cannot exist. Moore with all his faults might be esteemed; for he had no moral scrofula in his mind, no hopeless polluting taint, such, for instance, as that of falsehood; neither was he the slave of his appetites . . . he was a man undegraded, the disciple of Reason, NOT the votary of Sense. The same might be said of old Helstone . . . both might boast a valid claim to the proud title of "lord of the creation," for no animal vice was lord of them: they looked and were superior beings to poor Sykes. (S, pp. 103–104)

The abstract, low-key, logical quality of Austen's writing here is characteristic of her prose. Darcy and Bingley are the only concrete objects; adjectives and nouns are all first-level abstractions; none of the verbs are concrete. In contrast, Brontë's prose is a great deal more concrete and, concomitantly, a great deal more figurative. *Love, Meanness, Natural Affection, Sense,* and *Reason* are, of course, abstractions, but they are all personified: Love can *excuse*, Meanness can *kill* and *cripple*, Sense and Reason are gods who possess votaries and disciples. Animal vice is not personified by capitalization, yet it is human in that it can be *lord* of men. Meanness in turn is metaphorically *moral scrofula* and *polluting taint*; both Moore and Helstone are metaphorically disciples or votaries, and, allusively, *lords of creation.* The whole passage, in short, is imaginatively rather than literally stated; Austen might have said, "Moore, for all his faults, was neither dishonest nor unreasonable."

Without exception, the language of the *Pride and Prejudice* passage belongs to the sphere of social behavior; the easy, balanced syntax fortifies the narrator's civil and coolly rational tone. It is a language bare of metaphor because its scope of reference is intra-social. The manners and motivations of one character are explored in comparison with the manners and motivations of another: Darcy's behavior is less pleasing than Bingley's, for example; or Marianne's sensibility is more highly developed than Elinor's. An incident in Austen's last novel *Persuasion*, in many ways her most subjective work, aptly illustrates how foreign she still finds figurative thought. The narrator speaks of "the last smiles of the year upon the tawny leaves and withered hedges," then immediately disclaims any responsibility for such poetic nonsense by making it clear that these are the words of Anne Eliot, "repeating to herself some few of the thousand poetical descriptions extant of autumn, that season . . . which has drawn from every poet, worthy of being read, some attempt at description, or some lines of feeling" (*Persuasion* [Middlesex, Eng., 1965], p. 107). The narrator's ironical, conscious tone mocks Anne Eliot's sensibilities; we hear the echo of Elinor's dry remark to Marianne: "Is it not everyone who has your fondness for dead leaves."

The figurative language in the Brontë passage, on the other hand, by drawing heavily on Biblical allusion and personified abstractions, removes the issues from a social sphere and asserts the supremacy of man's moral nature over his social being. It would be difficult to tell from the apocalyptic tenor of the paragraph that it springs from a rather trivial scene of companionable and celebratory drinking. But Brontë possesses no social yardstick by which to measure her characters' actions; she has little tolerance, therefore, for the relative or the venial in human behavior. The actions of her characters are not judged by their viability, but are measured against such absolutes as reason, sense, imagination, feeling, truth, or nature.[1] Austen speaks of "the last smiles of the year" with irony, since to her humanistically oriented mind it is absurd to invest subordinate nature with human qualities. To Brontë, this figure of speech would come spontaneously, for if man can be interpreted imaginatively in his relationship to nature, nature conversely can be interpreted in its relationship to man.

1. Lucy Snowe is perhaps the only exception in her toleration of Madame Beck's devious ways of running the *pensionnat*, a toleration that ceases as Lucy changes from a passive to an active human being.

Antithesis is created, then, from the contrast between language and syntax. In another sense, antithesis—or tension—exists in Brontë's prose as an inevitable concomitant of all metaphoric language, which by definition involves the linking of disparate elements. Of course, this metaphoric "tension" can vary to a great degree. Brontë's metaphoric language has been called commonplace, and Rochester's endearments to Jane when she meets him in the rain on his return to Thornfield cited as evidence: Jane is "dripping like a mermaid," "slippery as an eel," "thorny as a briarfield," a "stray lamb" who has "wandered out of the fold to seek [her] shepherd." Metaphors used to describe Ginevra Fanshawe, for example, although fresh, are similarly unstartling. We are told that her love and hate are "mere cobwebs and gossamer," that in her "feathers" she is "a mere jay in borrowed plumes," that gaiety "expanded her butterfly's wings, lit up their gold-dust and bright spots, made her flash like a gem, and flush like a flower." Rochester's language, however, is appropriate to a man who makes no claim to being a poet, and a similar rationale can be found for the jay and butterfly metaphors that describe Ginevra: the commonplace here is suitable and effective, for it makes the point that Ginevra Fanshawe *is* common and trivial.

Nevertheless, if one were to conduct a kind of Cloze measure test on Brontë's metaphors by leaving the second half of the equation blank and asking literate people unfamiliar with her novels to guess at the contents of the missing half, there would probably be a higher rate of predictability for Brontë's metaphors than for, say, the metaphors of John Donne.[2] *Gem* is after all a more obvious conclusion to "flash like a —" than *stiff twin compasses* is to "they are two so as —." Yet Brontë's language strikes one as powerful and original; hardly diluted or ineffectual poeticized prose. I would suggest, therefore, that the intensity of her language derives less from tensions generated *within* individual figures of comparison by a yoking to-

2. Or, to use a term employed by linguists M. A. K. Halliday, John Spencer, and Michael J. Gregory, we could say that the terms of Brontë's metaphors often *collocate;* i.e., have a tendency to occur in the same linguistic environment.

gether of heterogeneous materials, than from tensions generated
between figures of comparison which are sharply antithetical.
That is, while little internal drama exists in a simile like "hands
cold as ice," a great deal of dramatic tension is created if this
simile is followed by the words, "tears hot as molten metal."
This conflict, of course, is not limited to figurative language,
but obtains whenever lexical items occur in contrast—hate and
love, for example, or imagination and reality—or in the frequent
oxymorons that in microcosm embody the broader antitheses of
Brontë's style: "gall-honey pleasure," "soft impeachment," "ten-
der pain," "soft tyranny," "grave joy," "envenomed pleasure,"
"earthly angel," "human flower," "gentle mutiny." The most significant approach to Charlotte Brontë's language, both literal
and figurative, therefore, is through structure: we must return
to the many instances of antithesis on all three structural levels
to discover more closely what quantities are juxtaposed and
what thematic patterns emerge.

II

Of the many elements that Brontë opposes, several occur with
such frequency that they must be acknowledged as the major
thematic preoccupations of the novels. These are the contrasts
between appearance and reality, privation and plenty, fetters
and freedom, passion and reason. The first of these, the problem
of determining the real from the seeming, is raised at varying
levels of significance in all the novels. The issue can be uncomplicated, like Crimsworth's discovery of the very un-ideal characters of the young ladies he once envisioned as angels: "I
cannot say I was chagrined or downcast by the contrast which
the reality of a pensionnat de demoiselles presented to my
vague ideal of the same community; I was only enlightened
and amused . . ." (*P*, p. 75). Again, the veil may be torn away
quickly, as in the case of Jane Eyre's accurate and quickly
achieved understanding of Blanche Ingram: "She was very
showy, but she was not genuine: she had a fine person, many

brilliant attainments; but her mind was poor, her heart barren by nature . . ." (*JE*, p. 176). With characters who have the guile to mask their real personalities, the task of discerning the real beneath the seeming is more difficult. Lucy Snowe comes to understand the real nature of Madame Beck only over a period of many months: "All this seemed very pleasant, and Madame appeared goodness itself . . . . Thus did the view appear, seen through the enchantment of distance; but there came a time when distance was to melt for me . . ." (*V*, p. 64). And Crimsworth discovers Mlle. Reuter's pernicious character only accidentally, having been deceived enough by her mild manner to consider making her his wife.

In *Shirley* and *Villette*, the failure of Caroline Helstone and Lucy Snowe to realize the truth behind the appearance has almost disastrous consequences. Caroline is led by the appearance of affection between Shirley and Robert Moore to assume that they are lovers, a tragic misinterpretation which brings on illness and almost leads to her death. In *Villette*, the problem of discerning real from false is even more acute, however; and because Lucy Snowe is twice the heroine Caroline is, we feel that Lucy's confusion of appearance and reality has far greater tragic potential than Caroline's. Part of Lucy's misfortune arises from other characters failing to discern *her* real nature: Dr. John and Paulina, for example, assume that Lucy enjoys vicariously sharing in their love prattle and thereby cause her untold pain. But self-deception injures Lucy more; and when on the fête night, after a series of misjudgments, Lucy mistakes M. Paul's ward for his intended bride, when she courageously takes to herself the painful "truth," we cannot but feel—to borrow a Brontëan metaphor—that the cup has been poisoned once too often; that she has suffered too much. Appearance and reality are of critical importance at one point in *Jane Eyre* when, after the interrupted wedding ceremony, Jane feels her confidence in Rochester betrayed: ". . . faith was blighted—confidence destroyed! Mr. Rochester was not to me what he had been; for he was not what I had thought him" (p. 281). But the central issue of *Jane Eyre* is less the problem of discerning the real from the seeming than the problem of determining right from wrong. The bias of *Jane Eyre* is moral; the bias of *Villette* epistemological: the latter is the more complex work of art.

In one sense, however, the problem of real and seeming necessarily lies at the heart of the first-person narrative. Lacking omniscience, unable to see into the minds of other characters, the protagonist must inevitably be involved in the process of discovering the real nature of those about him. Because Brontë's narrators relate events from the perspective of maturity, they have, of course, the prerogative of disclosing the truth immediately, and occasionally they do; exigencies of plot and theme, however, usually demand that the discovery of the reality disguised by appearance occupy a significant portion of the action. In one respect, the Brontë protagonist is ideally situated to make these discoveries: as an uncorrupted outsider, an observer rather than an actor on the social stage, the protagonist has the vantage of distance, skepticism, and integrity. On the other hand, this isolation breeds a naïveté and ignorance that can distort truth rather than reveal it: Lucy Snowe's misinterpretations are a case in point. Even more fundamentally, however, these first-person narratives involve the discovery—by others— of the superior character of the protagonist. The moral superiority of Crimsworth is acknowledged by his churlish brother, by Mlle. Reuter and by Pelet; and Jane triumphs over her childhood tormentors as well as over Rochester and St. John Rivers. Lucy Snowe, a more complicated character than Crimsworth or Jane, evolves into a spirited, capable, and passionate person rather than being revealed as such. It is a measure of Charlotte Brontë's maturer realism that she permits Lucy Snowe's character to remain unplumbed by people like Dr. John Bretton, Paulina, M. de Bassompierre, and Mrs. Bretton, who are ultimately judged inferior in mind and heart, however, by their failure to know the real Lucy Snowe. Besides, of course, M. Paul, only the unholy trio that surround him—Madame Beck, Père Silas, Madame Walravens—understand Lucy's real character. For this Lucy grants them a certain respect if not liking; her ironic salute to their prosperity comes as a fitting close to the novel; it is a gesture permitted one who has proven herself superior to her enemies and to fate.

This dichotomy of appearance and reality is expressed figuratively in images that distinguish between surface and depth, revealed or hidden. When Lucy comes to understand the sensual and indulgent nature that lies beneath Madame Beck's cool and controlled exterior, she is able to penetrate Madame's "disguise": her "mask," her "domino" becomes a "mere network reticulated with holes," and Lucy sees underneath "a being heartless, self-indulgent, ignoble." Blanche Ingram displays a "showy" and "brilliant" surface, but beneath it, her "mind [is] poor, her heart barren by nature." Crimsworth at first thinks Mlle. Reuter wise, charitable, and amiable; then the "plating of pretension" wears off and the "real material" appears below. Similarly, Pelet seems affable and mild on the surface, but Crimsworth detects "the existence of flint or steel under an external covering of velvet." The Brontë protagonist also wears "plating," but unlike the disguises of a Madame Beck or a Blanche Ingram, this armor serves as protection for the vulnerable and sensitive heart beneath. M. Pelet observes of Crimsworth: "Any woman sinking her shaft deep enough, will at last reach a fathomless spring of sensibility in thy breast, Crimsworth"; and Crimsworth himself describes his reaction to the *demoiselles* of the *pensionnat* in terms of girding on a protective armor: "In less than five minutes they had thus revealed to me their characters, and in less than five minutes I had buckled on a breast-plate of steely indifference, and let down a visor of impassible austerity" (*P*, pp. 79, 73).

When the depth of a Brontë protagonist *is* plumbed, we find, of course, neither barrenness nor heartlessness, but richness and sensibility. These qualities are often formulated in metaphors of hidden treasure:

> . . . at last, I am bound to confess it, her finger, essaying, proving every atom of the casket, touched its secret spring, and for a moment the lid sprung open; she laid her hand on the jewel within . . . . (*P*, p. 90)

"I need not sell my soul to buy bliss. I have an inward treasure, born with me, which can keep me alive if all extraneous delights should be withheld; or offered only at a price I cannot afford to give." (*JE*, p. 191)

"I may be communicative, yet know where to stop. In showing my treasure, I may withhold a gem or two—a curious unbought, graven stone—an amulet, of whose mystic glitter I rarely permit even myself a glimpse." (*S*, p. 354)

So speak Crimsworth, Rochester (of Jane), and Shirley, describing in terms of worldly value those priceless and inherent qualities with which the Brontë protagonist is endowed: feeling, integrity, self-esteem. And Lucy Snowe? In the novel which most frequently uses images of gems and precious metals to describe human qualities, the hidden-treasure image is applied not to Lucy but to Dr. John. Paulina has a magic, persuasive accent that opens a "scarce-known treasure-house" within Dr. John's character. Or, in respect to his mother, "the best treasure of Mrs. Bretton's life was certainly casketed in her son's bosom; her dearest pulse throbbed in his heart" (*V*, p. 160). As for Lucy, it is perhaps fitting that this most diffident of Brontë heroines should not claim gold or jewels for her hidden qualities, but should speak of her inner worth as true ore. This is what Paul Emanuel is privileged to find when, in that startling metaphor, he opens the eyelids of his student (another version of protective "plating") with "pitiless finger and thumb," and gazes deep through the pupil and the irids into the brain and into Lucy's very heart (*V*, p. 297). True ore, flashy dross; gold, clay; "the little cup of pure metal," "this gorgeous and massy vase of mosaic": these figures appear again and again, mingled with the buried-treasure motif, as symbols of the inner and the outer, the true and the false. Because of Lucy's ambiguous and fluctuating judgments of him, the real worth of Dr. John's character can be disputed. The figurative language of appearance and reality only intensifies its ambiguity: on the one hand, he is endowed with the precious "secret treasure-house" of the Brontë protagonist; on the other hand, a most damning judgment is couched in Lucy's seemingly innocent observation that she was driven to compare Dr. John's beamy, golden head "to that of the 'golden image' which Nebuchadnezzer the king had set up" (*V*, p. 84).

The modern reader cannot, I believe, overlook the rather obvious Freudian symbolism of the casket/treasure-house and buried-treasure images. Indeed, Brontë makes it very apparent that ultimately the casket may be associated with the body (or more specifically, the sexual organs) by herself identifying the buried treasure as "heart"—a word frequently synonymous in Brontë language with physical passion. This physical passion, or potential for love, remains hidden from the world, to be unearthed by only the sympathetic One. In Jane Eyre particularly, this unmined treasure is her chastity, the source of that self-esteem which can keep her alive "if all extraneous delights should be withheld; or offered at a price [she] cannot afford to give." One of Paul Emanuel's predominant characteristics is his chastity—any maiden would have been completely safe with him, Lucy tells us; and again this chastity or suppressed sexual passion is associated with the hidden-treasure image when we are told that long ago M. Paul had buried his passions.

The motif of buried treasure is dramatized several times in *Villette* in slightly different form. Lucy receives letters from Dr. John. These symbols of her passion for him—*not* his for her—she figuratively and literally buries: in a case, secreted in a locked box, hidden in a drawer. In the chapter "A Burial" she attempts to kill her feeling for Dr. John once and for all. Ceremoniously she rolls up the letters, symbols of passion, "untasted treasure," and thrusts them into a hermetically sealed jar. This jar she buries at the roots of the priapic tree, Old Methuselah, in the *allée défendue*, a walk designed to prohibit commerce between male and female students of the two schools. Minutes after she "hides her treasure," Lucy sees a "tall, sable-robed, snowy-veiled woman"—the nun, symbol of the denied sexuality that Lucy has just buried. Later when Lucy recalls that moonlight burial, the treasure image undergoes a bizarre change: *casket* becomes *coffin*, *buried gold* the *gold* of Dr. John's hair: "Was this feeling dead? I do not know, but it was buried. Sometimes I thought the tomb unquiet, and dreamed strangely of disturbed earth, and of hair, still golden, and living, obtruded through coffin-chinks" (V, p. 307).

The association of casket with coffin, of treasure with the rites of burial, suggests that Brontë's attitude is unconsciously ambiguous toward the hidden or reserved passions of her protagonists. On the one hand, the treasure is precious, too precious to be given away or even revealed. On the other hand, as the language of burial implies, the repression of passion is unnatural, deadly, a sentiment voiced by both Caroline Helstone and Jane Eyre, and enacted in the narrative of Lucy Snowe's stifled existence.[3] But, of course, the treasure symbol is not limited to physical passion: it may stand for sensibility, inner vitality or courage, or independence as well. In a broader sense, all Brontë protagonists lead, in Arnold's phrase, "buried lives." Alienated from ordinary social values, checked and bridled by poverty, caste, and sex, her heroes and heroines live unacknowledged by the world; the best part of their natures are disguised, held back, to be shown to the privileged few. In this enforced elitism resides both their weakness and their strength.

The antithesis of privation and plenty is seldom called just that in the novels; it is rather my term for a theme stated most frequently in figurative terms of starvation and nourishment or thirst and thirst quenched. It has been claimed that no novelist rivals Dickens in the quantites of food and drink consumed in his novels.[4] A counter-claim can be advanced: no author rivals Charlotte Brontë in the metaphorical quantities of food and drink either craved or consumed by her characters. Matthew

3. It is interesting that in the preface to the second edition of *Jane Eyre* Brontë characterizes appearance and reality in the same terms and also associates death and burial with this imagery: "The world may not like to see ideas dissevered, for it has been accustomed to blend them; finding it convenient to make *external show* pass for *sterling worth*—to let *whitewashed walls* vouch for *clean shrines*. It may hate him who dares to scrutinise and expose—to *rase the gilding*, and show *base metal under it* —to penetrate *the sepulchre*, and reveal *charnel relics* . . . ."

4. William Ross Clark, "The Hungry Mr. Dickens," in *Discussions of Charles Dickens*, ed. Clark (Boston, 1961), pp. 24–29.

Arnold was thus right when he spoke of Brontë's mind as containing nothing but hunger, rebellion, and rage. Dickens's characters gorge and imbibe; Brontë people raven after love, freedom, and hope, droop and decline when these are denied, snatch voraciously when they are offered.

Hunger language, for example, predominates in Brontë's description of Caroline Helstone's unrequited love for Robert Moore. When Moore is kind, then cold, Caroline suffers: ". . . a few minutes before, her famished heart had tasted a drop and crumb of nourishment, that, if freely given, would have brought back abundance of life where life was failing; but the generous feast was snatched from her, spread before another, and she remained but a bystander at the banquet" (S, p. 197). When Caroline is dying of a "famished heart," Brontë tells us: "Life wastes fast in such vigils . . . during which the mind—having no pleasant food to nourish it—no manna of hope—no hived-honey of joyous memories—tries to live on the meagre diet of wishes, and failing to derive thence either delight or support, and feeling itself ready to perish with craving want, turns to philosophy, to resolution, to resignation . . ." (p. 277). Caroline, however, is saved the terrible fate of withering into an old maid, those pathetic creatures that Brontë describes in language that links starvation to sexual hunger as "extenuated spectres," "ahungered and athirst to famine," to whom "a crumb is not thrown once a year" (p. 143).

When Brontë characters cannot get nourishment from salubrious sources, they turn to their sorrow and feed upon it. Jane leans over the crib of the dying Helen Burns, "devouring her tears"; when Lucy must part from Dr. John, she goes, "swallowing her tears as if they had been wine." Or they swallow deadly nourishment—poison. Thus Jane Eyre says of her supposedly hopeless love for Rochester that she had "surfeited herself on sweet lies and swallowed poison as if it were nectar." At her most reckless, the Brontë protagonist welcomes poison, which, if its kills, seems to offer relief from the pangs of sexual and emotional starvation in the process. Such a bane is Graham Bretton's superficial affection for Lucy, cherished despite its deadliness: "'. . . be it poison or food, you cannot, at least, deny its own delicious quality—sweetness. Better, perhaps, to die quickly a pleasant death, than drag on long a charmless life'" (V, p. 199).

In *Villette* the language of hunger and thirst dominates. The antithesis of privation and plenty, besides providing the organizing principle of the novel, thus provides also its central metaphor, thereby binding the language of the narrative firmly to its structure. Lucy Snowe consistently translates her life of privation into metaphor of starvation or thirst, her moments of gratification into metaphor of nourishment or thirst quenched. These images chart the course of Lucy's developing personality: while her existence fluctuates painfully between want and gratification, her capacity to resist pain and to actively pursue pleasure grows steadily. At first Lucy's life is so barren that she is satisfied to live vicariously, nourished only by her imagination: ". . . I seemed to hold two lives—the life of thought, and that of reality; and, provided the former was nourished with a sufficiency of the strange necromantic joys of fancy, the privileges of the latter might remain limited to daily bread, hourly work, and a roof of shelter" (p. 65). When Lucy is coincidentally reunited with her childhood friends, the Bretton family, she cannot help for the first time in her adult life contemplating the real pleasures friendship might offer her; yet she holds herself sternly in check: "'. . . let me be content with a temperate draught of this living stream: let me not run athirst, and apply passionately to its welcome waters: let me not imagine in them a sweeter taste than earth's fountains know'" (p. 153).

After experiencing the happiness of Dr. John Bretton's benevolent if careless friendship, Lucy grows even less satisfied with dreams and fancies. With characteristic Brontëan avidity, she longs for a "perennial spring" to slake her emotional thirst even while her rational faculties continue to caution her against expecting further affectionate attentions from Dr. John. Reason tells her plainly that she cannot hope for Dr. John's love, but Lucy cries out against the stint of reality, reminding herself that Reason has given her only "barren board," or flung her for sustenance "the gnawed bone dogs had forsaken." Imagination, on the other hand, in allowing her to dream has appeased her hunger "with food, sweet and strange, gathered amongst gleaning angels, garnering their dew-white harvest in the first fresh hour of a heavenly day . . ." (p. 197). Lacking the temerity to trust yet that reality might offer her plenty instead of privation, Lucy clings to Imagination, which has nourished her in the past.

When a letter does arrive from Dr. John, Lucy is overwhelmed by this tangible evidence of affection. In what proves the turning point of her life, she recognizes that real joy far transcends imagined pleasure, that Imagination is indeed "for mortals deadly." Again Lucy's emotional satisfaction is expressed in terms of hunger and nourishment:

> I held in my hand a morsel of real solid joy: not a dream, not an image of the brain, not one of those shadowy chances imagination pictures, and on which humanity starves but cannot live; not a mess of that manna I drearily eulogized a while ago . . . an aliment divine, but for mortals deadly. It was neither sweet hail, nor small coriander seed—neither slight wafer, nor luscious honey, I had lighted on; it was the wild, savoury mess of the hunter, nourishing and salubrious meat, forest-fed or desert-reared, fresh, healthful, and life-sustaining. (p. 205)

Paul Emanuel guesses Lucy's attachment to Dr. John and suggests that it is not "salubrious" but "sweet poison," a judgment with which Lucy eventually concurs. As her affection for M. Paul grows, the language of hunger and thirst appropriately abates; the "sweet poison" variation of the motif recurs, however, at the climax of the novel, the attempt of Madame Beck and her satellites to sever the relationship of Paul and Lucy. In her dormitory room Lucy warns Madame Beck to leave her because in her hand there is "chill and poison"; Lucy, however, finally drinks from the "poisoned cup." Paradoxically this time the poison or drug *is* sweet: instead of unconsciousness it brings Lucy to life, for wandering through the village under its influence, she sees M. Paul with his "bride" and is forced for the first time to admit the depths of her love for him. While this event constitutes the climax of the novel, the hunger-nourishment motif reappears in the dénouement when Lucy says of

M. Paul's letters, as she had said of Dr. John's, "They were real food that nourished, living water that refreshed"; and finally with terrible irony to describe the tragedy of Paul Emanuel's death: "That storm . . . did not cease till the Atlantic was strewn with wrecks: it did not lull till the deeps had gorged their full of sustenance" (p. 416).

The Biblical nature of this figurative language with its talk of "manna," "sweet hail," "slight wafer," and "living stream" is, of course, obvious. Similarly significant, I believe, is the fact that the characters in the novels seldom eat anything (figuratively and literally) but liquid—tea, water, wine—and bread. The bread and wine of communion is strongly suggested, and with it, the desire that this purely symbolic sustenance be transmuted into the reality: body and blood. This religious, symbolic language has nothing to do with a longing for God, however: it is tangible, earthly love that Lucy hungers for; she is sick of "divine aliment," a food "on which humanity starves but cannot live." Food and drink, bread and wine, indeed represent salvation and regeneration of the spirit, but they symbolize a salvation and regeneration found only in human relationships. J. Hillis Miller has seen correctly that in the Victorian novel God is dead and relationships between man and man are stressed in an attempt to satisfy religious longings in a world where relations to God are blocked.[5] In Brontë's novels God exists, but is not immanent: "Certainly, at some hour," says Lucy Snowe with controlled despair, "though perhaps not YOUR hour, the waiting water will stir . . . the healing herald will descend. The cripple and the blind, and the dumb, and the possessed, will be led to bathe. Herald, come quickly! Thousands lie round the pool, weeping and despairing, to see it, through slow years, stagnant" (V, pp. 153–154). In the absence of a present God, the Brontë protagonist substitutes temporarily

---

5. J. Hillis Miller, *The Form of Victorian Fiction* (Notre Dame, 1968), p. 96. Unlike the novelists Miller discusses (Dickens, Trollope, Eliot, Hardy), Brontë is not a social novelist, nor, concomitantly, a novelist who excludes man's relation to physical nature or to a supernatural power. Her protagonists are not defined by their relationship to others but by subjective standards.

the deity of Imagination to sustain her but finds herself starving on "sick fancy": it is human, physical love she craves. This craving, as we have seen, is frequently expressed in religious terms, creating a peculiar tension between the claims of body and spirit which the socially oriented novels of Thackeray, Eliot, and Trollope, for example, completely lack.

Like the metaphoric variations played upon the theme of appearance and reality, corollaries exist for the privation and plenty antithesis too. A frequent variation is the juxtaposition of illness and health: when Brontë characters are deprived of love—that is, food—this famine leads to illness. Illness and health are in turn often described in terms of waste and bloom: if the soil is barren, her characters, like plants, wither and fade. All four metaphors—illness, health, waste, bloom—are at play in Jane Eyre's lament over her dashed hopes, with the addition of the subtle juxtaposition of virgin (death) and woman (life):

> Jane Eyre, who had been an ardent, expectant woman— almost a bride—was a cold, solitary girl again . . . . A Christmas frost had come at midsummer; a white December storm had whirled over June . . . . My hopes were all dead—struck with a subtle doom, such as, in one night, fell on all the first-born in the land of Egypt. I looked on my cherished wishes, yesterday so blooming and glowing; they lay stark, chill, livid corpses, that could never revive. (*JE*, pp. 280–281)

This illness / wither—health / bloom motif is particularly persistent in *Shirley*, where it alternates with the famine / food opposition to describe Caroline Helstone's blighted hopes of Robert Moore's love. Finding his niece changed, "the rose . . . dwindled and faded to a mere snowdrop: bloom . . . vanished, flesh wasted," her insensitive uncle is moved to observe: " 'These women are incomprehensible. . . . To-day you see them bouncing, buxom, red as cherries, and round as apples; to-morrow they exhibit themselves effete as dead weeds, blanched and broken down'" (*S*, p. 151). Or the antithesis is between winter and spring: ". . . the heaviness of a broken spirit, and of pining and palsying faculties, settled slow on her bouyant youth. Winter seemed conquering her spring: the mind's soil

and its treasures were freezing gradually to barren stagnation"
(S, pp. 146–147).

Because the fetters / freedom antithesis constitutes a portion
of the discussion of *Jane Eyre* in the next chapter, it can be
dealt with rather briefly here. There is a distinction drawn in
all four novels between different kinds of fetters and different
kinds of freedom. That is, there is always the stipulation—and
it is nothing new with Brontë—that man can be free in captivity
and fettered in freedom; that, in Lucy Snowe's words, ". . .
peril, loneliness, an uncertain future, are not oppressive evils,
so long . . . as Liberty lends us her wings, and Hope guides us
by her star" (V, p. 48). In a Brontë novel to be constrained by
poverty or toil is always preferable to being enslaved by forfeiting one's standards: one is mere physical or mental torture; the
other moral degradation. The distinction is drawn so clearly in
The Professor that the passages must be quoted. For Crimsworth, work is a yoke, but an honorable one. On the other hand,
Mlle. Reuter's sensual passion for him is slavish and enslaving:

> I, a bondsman just released from the yoke, freed for one week
> from twenty-one years of constraint, must, of necessity, resume
> the fetters of dependency. Hardly had I tasted the delight of
> being without a master when duty issued her stern mandate:
> "Go forth and seek another service." I never linger over a pain-
> ful and necessary task. . . . (P, p. 48)

> I had ever hated a tyrant; and, behold, the possession of a
> slave, self-given, went near to transform me into what I abhor-
> red! There was at once a sort of low gratification in receiving
> this luscious incense from an attractive and still young wor-
> shipper; and an irritating sense of degradation in the very ex-
> perience of the pleasure. When she stole about me with the
> soft step of a slave, I felt at once barbarous and sensual as
> a pasha. (P, p. 162)

The word *slave* (and, concomitantly, *idol*) is a favorite of
Brontë's and is applied freely to anyone whose interests are
engaged solely through the senses rather than through the
"higher feelings." And slavery is a state to which many of her
characters must confess. In the nobler characters, the slave

state is transitory: a kind of sojourn in Vanity Fair that better prepares them for an earthly Celestial City. Such a lapse is Crimsworth's fleeting attraction to Mlle. Reuter, Rochester's Continental fling, Graham Bretton's fascination with Ginevra Fanshawe, St. John Rivers's attraction to Rosamond Oliver, even Lucy Snowe's love for Dr. John. The meaner characters never leave Vanity Fair: this company includes Edward Crimsworth, Mlle. Reuter, Pelet, Mrs. Reed, Georgiana Reed, Blanche Ingram, Zélie St. Pierre, Ginevra, the Count de Hamal, Père Silas—and alas! even the worthy Madame Beck.[6] On the other hand, nothing is less desirable than to be free from the bonds of real love; love "furnace-tried by pain, stamped by constancy, consolidated by affection's pure and durable alloy, submitted by intellect to intellect's own tests, and finally wrought up, by his own process, to his own unflawed completeness" (V, p. 395). Lucy Snowe's rationalized "'here I stand—free'" is quickly followed by the wry, "Nothing remained now but to take my freedom to my chamber . . . and see what I could make of it" (V, p. 394). The acknowledgment that real love is worth the risk of commitment, of forfeiting the freedom not to care, culminates the education of Lucy Snowe.

Apart from love, the freedom demanded by Brontë characters is modest enough: liberty means that while the protagonist can compromise to some extent with the Establishment, there must be no compromising of the protagonist's integrity and pride. Louis Moore, for example, is not free. His excessive hauteur and reserve are the result of trying to maintain his dignity in a family that does not acknowledge tutors as human beings. Caroline Helstone is not free, for she is spurned in love and has no other occupation through which she can achieve a sense of identity; she lives uselessly, fettered and buried in Briarfield Rectory, a place that reminds Rose Yorke of "a windowed grave." In that Madame Beck recognizes Lucy's pride and in-

6. In all the novels, Catholicism is equated with sensuality: Adèle is the illegitimate Catholic daughter of a *demimondaine;* in both *The Professor* and *Villette* the native Catholic Belgians are portrayed as blatantly sensual and stupid; Madame Beck is a sensualist as noted above; Père Silas is not a bad man, but degraded in his worship of the trappings of Rome.

dividuality, Lucy is free: for faithful service in a particular crisis, Madame rewards the other teachers with money; upon Lucy she bestows her trust—no mean gift. But let us add a stipulation: the freedom demanded may be modest enough—a schoolroom, homage to the *amour-propre*, the right to eccentricity—but the demands, as both the quantity and the quality of the freedom / fetters language reveals, are not modest; they are fierce and unceasing.

While a careful distinction has been drawn here between these three sets of antitheses, ultimately they are not discrete at all, but are merged in the author's mind. Appearance, privation, and fetters on the one hand, reality, plenty, and freedom on the other, can be reduced to an ultimate antithesis: life, or death-in-life. Besides the obvious thematic affinity of these antitheses, the evidence for connecting them is verbal, based on the principle that if one assigns the same word to two different objects, these objects are somehow linked in one's mind. And Brontë inevitably describes one antithesis in terms of another. Thus in *Shirley*, the appearance / reality motif is stated in terms of illness and health, a variant of privation / plenty: ". . . breaking day dimmed the creation of Fancy . . . . The shape that, seen in a moonbeam, lived, had a pulse, had movement, wore health's glow and youth's freshness, turned cold and ghostly grey . . . . It wasted" (S, p. 203). Similarly in *Villette*, reality is associated with food or plenty. Lucy's letter from Dr. John is depicted as real substance, or treasure, as opposed to Lucy's dreams. Lucy *feasts* her eyes on this letter, and then locks it up without having read "the untasted treasure." When she opens it later, the hunger language reappears: "I held in my hand a morsel of real solid joy." When the letters cease to arrive, Lucy's devastation is described in the merged language of fetters, hunger, and appearance: "I suppose animals kept in cages, and so scantily fed as to be always upon the verge of famine, await their food as I awaited a letter." Trying to take comfort, Lucy re-reads the old letters: "I . . . feasted on my crust from the Barmecide's loaf. It did not nourish me: I pined on it . . . my gold was withering to leaves before my eyes, and I was sorrowing over the disillusion . . ." (*V*, pp. 217, 229). Freedom is frequently described in terms of food, fetters in terms of starvation: Brontë characters *thirst* for liberty like Louis Moore, or like Crimsworth, "*taste* the delight of being without a master." This connection between food and freedom is fortified when Brontë states: "The world can understand well enough the process of perishing for want of food: perhaps few persons can enter into or follow out that of going mad from solitary confinement" (*V*, p. 234). And finally, reality is associated with freedom, illusion with bondage: when Crimsworth, Rochester, and Dr. John discover the true natures of Mlle. Reuter, Céline, and Ginevra Fanshawe respectively, they cease being slaves; and Lucy Snowe's assertion that truth strips away falsehood and leaves one free forms a crucial component of the Brontë creed. The clustering of these mingling motifs in so many crucial and memorable scenes of the novels (scenes made memorable *because* of this language) identifies them, I believe, as dominant themes of Brontë's fiction.

On which pan of the balance does Charlotte Brontë place reason, or its frequent antithesis, passion? Certainly the dichotomy is an important one; in Robert Martin's opinion, for example, the study of the adjustment between the reason and the passions is the major theme of all the novels.[7] Without wishing to confuse the issue needlessly, it must be said that the antithesis is not always that clear-cut; that is, the quantity weighed against reason is not always passion. When it is, the issue—in the author's conscious mind at least—is simple enough: reason or judgment must dominate. Thus Crimsworth summons the physician Reason to cure him of his physical attraction to Zoraïde Reuter; the "gypsy" approves in Platonic metaphor the fact that in Jane's forehead, " 'Reason sits firm and holds the reins, and she will not let the feelings burst away and hurry her to wild chasms.' " Similarly, Robert Moore must be esteemed because he is "a man undegraded, the disciple of Reason, NOT the votary of Sense" (*P*, p. 98; *JE*, p. 191; *S*, p. 104).

7. Robert Martin, *The Accents of Persuasion* (London, 1966), p. 40.

When reason is juxtaposed with sexual passion unrelieved by
emotional attachment, or with irrational behavior, therefore,
passion must be weighed along with appearance, privation, and
fetters as an element that degrades man; reason as a quality
that elevates him—and it is hardly surprising that Charlotte
Brontë should officially take this time-honored stand. Shirley's
mermaid, as we have seen, is perhaps the most striking symbol
of the dual nature of man. Elsewhere, the phallic, amphibian
body of the mermaid is replaced by the obviously equivalent
metaphor of the snake, and is applied to characters who are
ruled by sensuality. Zélie St. Pierre is profligate: "That little
quality showed its snake-head to me but once, peeping out very
cautiously. A curious kind of reptile it seemed . . ." (V, p. 108).
Lucy Snowe's final revelation of Madame Beck's character exposes her as a sensualist, but the snake images associated with
her throughout could have warned us of her hidden nature
even without Lucy's direct accusation: in her attempts to at-
tach Paul Emanuel to herself solely through selfish motives, she
is the serpent in the Eden Lucy struggles so desperately to at-
tain. The sexual jealousy Rochester feels at discovering his
mistress with another lover is symbolized aptly by the phallic
snake: " '. . . I seemed to hear a hiss, and the green snake of
jealousy, rising on undulating coils from the moonlit balcony,
glided within my waistcoat, and ate its way in two minutes to
my heart's core' " (JE, p. 137). The young gentlemen, invited
by Madame Beck to her fête but prohibited from coming any-
where near the young ladies by Madame, who sketches "a sort
of cordon" around them, are again sexual temptation in para-
dise, and indeed Brontë describes them humorously as fasci-
nating and dangerous young rattlesnakes (V, p. 123).

But frequently it is not passion that Brontë juxtaposes with
reason, but feeling, or (it is the same) heart with brain; and
then, if a choice is necessary—they are best united—feeling
is the quality that invariably wins Brontë's sympathy. Mlle.
Reuter's staple ingredient is abstract reason: "no Tallyrand was
ever more passionless than Zoraïde Reuter"; and we know what
her creator thought of this character. On the other hand, we

can guess which side Brontë takes when Frances Henri argues against Yorke Hunsden that it is " 'better to be without logic than without feeling' " (*P*, pp. 76, 212). Like Zoraïde Reuter, Madame Beck has a shrewd mind, but a heart of stone: her eye never knows "the fire which is kindled in the heart or the softness which flows thence" (*V*, p. 61). By the same criterion, Shirley condemns the poet Milton, for although his vision was vast, he lacked intuitive sympathy: " 'Cary, we are alone: we may speak what we think. Milton was great, but was he good? His brain was right; how was his heart?' " (*S*, p. 252). Again, St. John Rivers has intellect, but no heart with which to give or receive affection, so that, bitterly, Jane tells him she will give her heart to God since he has so little use for it. Ideally, both brain and heart are sound, active, and true. It is significant in the light of the ambiguity of Dr. John's character that he stands damned with faint praise on both counts: "Dr. John COULD think, and think well, but he was rather a man of action than of thought; he COULD feel, and feel vividly in his way, but his heart had no chord for enthusiasm . . ." (*V*, p. 222). If striking evidence is needed of Brontë's preference for feeling, rather than brain, there is the fact that the word *heart* appears over six hundred and fifty times in the four novels, indicating not only a preference for this organ of feeling, but an obsession with it.[8]

The dichotomy shifts again in *Villette*. When the antithesis between reason and passion *is* drawn, the reference is to a minor theme: Dr. John and Ginevra, for example; or Lucy's temptation to Catholicism, which is unequivocally identified with the sensual, while Protestantism with its "severely pure aspect" is reason's champion. No, the principal conflict in *Villette* is between the reason and the imagination. In this new dichotomy lies the chief distinction between *Jane Eyre* and Charlotte Brontë's last novel. Compared with Lucy Snowe, Jane is an active, simpler, more forthright person. Similarly, she is faced

---

8. The count includes derivatives like *hearty, heartless, heartsease,* etc., as well as *coeur* and about twenty-five instances of *cordial,* included as a cognate.

with simpler, more forthright alternatives: passion or prudence?
adultery or moral rectitude? The choice, for a Jane, is not intolerably difficult. On the other hand, Lucy Snowe lives a buried
life, a life of the mind, to use Colby's phrase, in which decisions
are more difficult since their results, unexternalized, cannot be
condemned or applauded by society. Rochester at one point
asks Jane who will be hurt if she lives with him unwed. The
answer is clear: Jane would be hurt; besides loss of self-esteem,
the servants would gossip, the clergy condemn, the neighbor-
ing squirearchy disapprove. However, whether Lucy Snowe
chooses to live in the world of the imagination or face the bleak
harshness of the real world, no one will be the wiser. Lucy's
temptation to desert the dictates of reason is so much the
greater.

As heart is preferred before brain, the evidence of *Villette*
must lead us to conclude that imagination has stronger claims
upon Lucy's soul than reason. It is with great effort that Lucy
leaves her "watch-tower of the nursery" for the classes below:
she would much prefer to shrink into her sloth like a snail in
a shell; to subsist on the nourishment "of the strange necromantic joys of fancy." And, although Lucy progresses toward
reality, toward rational involvement in life, the dreariness of
her existence demands that imagination be heard until the happiness of real affection replaces it. In a crux of the novel, Lucy
apostrophizes Imagination, "our sweet Help, our Divine Hope,"
and protests bitterly against "this hag, this Reason":

> Long ago I should have died of her ill-usage: her stint, her
> chill, her barren board, her icy bed, her savage, ceaseless blows;
> but for the kinder Power who holds my secret and sworn
> allegiance. . . . Divine, compassionate, succourable influence!
> When I bend the knee to other than God, it shall be at thy
> white and winged feet, beautiful on mountain or on plain.
> (V, p. 197)

"My secret and sworn allegiance." For Lucy, for Charlotte
Brontë, reason is indeed admirable, but limited, and as the
privation language of the passage indicates, associated with

death-in-life. Imagination, apostrophized in language that re-calls Milton's creating Spirit, is given to man to conquer earthly pain. This does not mean, of course, that imaginary joys are preferable to real ones: when Lucy receives Dr. John's letter, she calls it "a morsel of real solid joy: not a dream, not an image of the brain," and Caroline Helstone "starves on the meagre diet of wishes." Imagination offers mere substance com-pared to the nourishment of real pleasure; however, unlike un-flattering and unyielding reason, it makes a barren life bearable.

It seems an oversimplification, then, to label Brontë's novels primarily studies of the conflicting claims of reason versus the passions. The subject that lies at the heart of Brontë's fiction is rather, I believe, the more general problem of asserting and maintaining one's identity in a world that functions upon dif-ferent and chiefly hostile sets of values. The debate over reason and passion or imagination or feeling is only one aspect of that problem, as is Brontë's preoccupation with appearance and reality, with fetters and freedom, with privation and plenty. How, as an alien in society, is one to survive with integrity? Since the world is largely indifferent to the protagonist's fate, shall one obey one's heart and instinct, or still be bound by conscience? How is one to deal with suffering, and—more diffi-cult—with happiness? What constitutes freedom and independ-ence and how can they be maintained from a dependent and socially inferior position? What values are apparent and what values are real? As the Brontë heroine grapples with these is-sues, she solves the problem of establishing her identity: the end of the novels find the heroine or hero confirmed both by herself and society as an individual worthy of respect and admiration.[9]

9. Because his experiences follow this pattern, Louis Moore—not Shirley nor Caroline Helstone—is the natural hero of *Shirley*, even though his role is minor compared to Caroline, Shirley, or Robert Moore's. Brontë held back on her favorite theme of tutor and pupil, not expanding on Louis Moore until almost the last third of the novel; once his story is underway, however, his fate overshadows the rest. This shifting of focus is what makes *Shirley* such an unsatisfying novel: the reader's sympathy and attention are constantly being misled.

To describe Brontë's language as metaphoric, however, is to tell but half a tale. Equally characteristic is her use throughout all four novels of abstract personification. Inga-Stina Ewbank views this figurative phenomenon as a self-conscious literary device occurring as a result of a thorough acquaintance with eighteenth-century descriptive poetry.[10] Certainly Brontë was intimately acquainted with eighteenth-century poetry and prose; certainly the spirit of Augustan rationality as well as the unbinding of that rationality influenced her prose. If the many appeals to memory, imagination, conscience, prudence, and reason can be linked with any literary source, however, they are most aptly associated with that work very frequently alluded to in the novels—*The Pilgrim's Progress*. But it would be superficial to suggest that Charlotte Brontë was merely imitating Bunyan's form: if she uses abstract personifications like Bunyan, it is because her vision of life corresponded to his vision so that she could express that vision in similar terms. For each writer, life was perhaps best likened to a hazardous journey along roads fraught with peril, temptation, and pain. Both envisioned these perils as essentially abstract evils which could be battled by the adherence of the traveller to equally abstract virtues like duty, perseverance, or fortitude. Both possessed a seriousness of purpose and duty that often resulted in didacticism. And both substituted moral judgment for psychological understanding: Bunyan consistently, Brontë when delineating characters she did not really understand. Not possessing the mysticism Bunyan makes apparent in *Grace Abounding*, Charlotte Brontë places even more reliance upon ethical principles. In her fiction, the importance of these principles is further magnified by the isolation of the protagonist. In the absence of family and friends or flesh and blood foes, the protagonist's imagination clothes these abstractions in the flesh of near-reality: to them he turns for guidance or support; against them he protests and struggles. In the absence of a present God, the

10. Inga-Stina Ewbank, *Their Proper Sphere* (London, 1966), p. 180.

Brontë protagonist elevates principle to godhood: principle becomes the deity to which he sacrifices and prays. Crimsworth makes this idolatry patent:

> . . . the work of copying and translating business-letters—was a dry and tedious task enough, but had that been all . . . I should have set up the image of Duty, the fetish of Perseverance, in my small bedroom . . . and they two should have been my household gods, from which my darling, my cherished-in-secret Imagination, the tender and the mighty, should never . . . have severed me. (*P*, p. 23)

To a great extent, this interior action, this conflict between temptation and principle, substitutes in Brontë's novels for the external conflicts around which the novel, to this date, has centered. To a great extent also, the contrast between the relatively tame exterior lives of the characters (Jane Eyre's is perhaps an exception) and the violence of this interior drama creates the drama of a Brontë novel and lends to her fiction the "larger-than-life" quality frequently noted. Brontë's language may indeed suggest a self-conscious striving for effect, but the thematic centrality of the personifications and the fact that they are often the foci for the most intense moments in the novels indicate that this device is not artificially and consciously rhetorical, but a spontaneous formal expression of the author's view of reality itself.

Among other facets of Brontë's language that create the impression of forcefulness, are two which seem particularly important. The first is Charlotte Brontë's conspicuous use of archaisms and/or poeticisms. Thus, *sable* often appears for *black*; *eld* for *old*; *bark* for *ship*; *clime* for *climate*; *bourne* for *destination*; *flood* for *river*. *Ere* is invariably substituted for *before*; *e'en* for *even*; then there are whole spates of archaic or poetic oddities sprinkled throughout the pages: *athirst, avaunt, betime, erst, ever and anon, fain, methinks, thereanent, yclept* mingling with words like *beclouded, beseemed,* and *bethink* which are not properly archaic, but which have that flavor because of the Old English prefix. Or, Brontë will take poetic license with word forms, in poeticisms like *stilly, massy,* or *jetty*, or in phrases such as *full shining, full sure, waxing bright, roaming fitful*. The source of this language is no mystery considering Brontë's devotion to literature in general and to the late eighteenth-century and early Romantic poets in particular, but its extensive and serious use in novels which have a near-contemporary rather than an archaic setting surely is unique.

Another characteristic of the language strongly contributing to its emotional quality is its violence. Sometimes the hyperbole, the drama, is preposterous, inflating the event to such proportions that the reader's sympathies are lost and the effect is melodrama or even burlesque, although Brontë may have intended the tone to be satirical. Perhaps nothing in the novels is as ludicrous as William Crimsworth's dread upon receiving an invitation to tea from old Madame Pelet. "Surely she is not going to make love to me?" he asks himself, and the thought is so terrible that it calls forth language more appropriate for meeting with a Gorgon than with an old woman:

> There was a *fearful dismay* in this suggestion of *my excited imagination*, and if I had allowed myself time to dwell upon it, I should no doubt have cut there and then, *rushed back* to my chamber, and *bolted myself in*; but whenever a *danger or a horror* is *veiled with uncertainty*, the primary wish of the mind is to ascertain first the *naked truth*, reserving the expedient of *flight* for the moment when its *dread anticipation* shall be realized. I turned the door handle, and in an instant had crossed *the fatal threshhold . . . .* Already *the cold sweat started on my brow . . . .* (*P*, pp. 60–61)

More often, the drama intended is achieved. Lucy's journey to her ship, the *Vivid* ("Down the sable flood we glided . . . ."), the evening at the theater in *Villette*, impress us more like luridly tinged spectacles from Dante's "Inferno" than episodes in the life of a quiet and plain English girl. Similarly, military terms (they occur frequently in all the novels) turn Jane Eyre's confrontation with Mrs. Reed or Lucy Snowe's first day in the classroom into pitched battles fought to the last man. Lucy enters a room full of students prepared for her *overthrow*;

Blanche, Virginie, and Angélique *open the campaign; the revolt grows and spreads rife through the mutinous mass.* Lucy manages to silence *the leaders,* but one girl perseveres in *the riot,* a girl with *a dark, sinister, mutinous eye:* Lucy in *an unexpected attack, wrestles* with her; *the conflict* is brief; she locks her in the closet (*V,* pp. 68–69). A Belgian schoolroom? Or the barricades?

But this is relatively tame stuff. Brontë novels are written from a low pain threshhold, and the language of aggression mixes with the language of suffering. If the word *heart* occurs more than six hundred and fifty times in the novels, the word *blood* must occur almost as frequently, for invariably these hearts are *stabbed, pierced, torn, broken, wrung, penetrated, throbbed, rent, corroded, heaved, scalded, scorched, killed, strained, gnawed, crushed, shattered,* or *racked.* The nerves fare little better: they *thrill, shriek, pulsate, tremble, quiver,* and *scream.* In more extended metaphors, scorpions are squeezed until the hand and arm have swelled and quivered long with torture; recollections lacerate like tiny pen knives; hope is torn by the roots out of a riven heart; Conviction nails Certainty upon Lucy Snowe and fixes it with the strongest spikes her strongest strokes can drive; cheeks are scalded with tears like molten metal; vultures sink beak and talons into the side; and in that most terrible of images, a nail is driven through the throbbing temples and the head forced to turn upon it. Reason may control the novels thematically and structurally, but passion and violence dominate the language of Brontë's fiction.

By now, however, we could guess that to call Charlotte Brontë's language emotive is but to half tell a tale. A contradiction can be found within the language itself, for Brontë's language contains elements antithetical to the emotional and to the concreteness, particularity, and figurativeness which create it; elements associated with pedantry rather than with imaginative fervor, with journalism rather than with poeticized prose. Frequently, for example, there is a straining after erudition and variety that is almost painful. Perhaps the most flagrant instance occurs in the first chapter of *Shirley.* The opening concerns, it will be remembered, the "shower of curates" recently

fallen upon northern England. This in itself is a felicitous metaphor, but during the course of the chapter the reader is treated
to no less than thirty-one variations upon the names of the
curates Malone, Donne, and Sweeting. They must be seen to
be believed: an abundant shower; that affluent rain; vigorous
young colleague from Cambridge or Oxford; successors of the
apostles; disciples of Dr. Pusey; tools of the propaganda; pre-
ordained, specially sanctified successors of St. Paul, St. Peter,
and St. John; the precious plant; rods of Aaron; brethren; gentlemen; youthful Levites; young parsons; college lads; locusts;
apostles; presumptuous Babylonish masons; bad boys; native
of the land of shamrocks and potatoes; priestly Paddy; Irish
Peter; native of a conquered land; the isolated Hibernian; great
satrap of Egypt; angry old women; little David; spotless Joseph;
"Captain"; big, vacant Saph; little minstrel; and great, floun-
dering Saul.

There is a reason, if not an excuse, for this particular straining after novelty. Publishers and public waiting expectantly
after the great success of *Jane Eyre*, it was a critical moment
for Charlotte Brontë. At all costs she wished to be striking,
witty if possible; to initiate a more worldly and learned tone
to confirm her status as a newly famous author and to match
the broader scope of her third novel. The result, as we see, is
the unwieldy and self-consciously allusive mass of biblical, his-
torical, and religious variations on the word *curates*. But the
same tendency, less flagrant, can be marked in all the novels,
for frequently the author falls victim to what Fowler calls the
most incurable vice of the second-rate writer—the elegant variation. Thus, if *sky* occurs at one point, *welkin* is sure to follow;
azure succeeds *blue*; *equipage* follows *carriage*. When Jane
secures food from the kitchen at Thornfield, this food is called
within a few paragraphs *booty, cargo of victualage, dinner, this
forage*, and *our repast*. This straining for variety (although, admittedly, one does not always feel it as a strain) is all the more
interesting because it contradicts Brontë's propensity to use
certain words like *genial, suave, penetrate, blood, cordial, irids,
ray*, and, of course, *heart* with a frequency that is almost hyp-
notic. In this respect, her word choice confirms the ambivalent

propensities for both passion and restraint already noted in other characteristics of her style: the elegant variation is almost certainly a highly conscious and therefore restrained facet of her art; the reiterated words reflect the natural and spontaneous bent of her mind.

Another language trait perhaps consonant with the elegant variation is Charlotte Brontë's use of the "big" word or Latinism. Rhetoricians divide about big words: does forceful, effective writing result from the predominance of short, concrete, Anglo-Saxon words or from a more abstract polysyllabic vocabulary? The first may be argued to be more concrete and therefore more vivid; the second to have greater resonance, weight, and duration and therefore more impressiveness. Perhaps the greatest writers, like Shakespeare, are free with both. At any rate, Charlotte Brontë's prose is weighted with formal or pedantic language: Brontë characters do not *climb, ask, go, keep, see, read, die, talk, lead, name,* or *enter* but instead *ascend, inquire, depart, retain, behold, peruse, expire, confabulate, conduct, denominate,* or *penetrate.* Often a ponderous impressiveness is generated by this diction. At other times, it seems almost incredible that the author who created the spirited dialogue between Jane and "the gypsy," for example, or Ginevra Fanshawe and Lucy Snowe could put into Louis Moore's mouth a line like, "Does not the apparition make vividly manifest the obtuse mould of my heavy traits?" Or invent a ponderous circumlocution like this observation of Jane's: "I saw a universal manifestation of discontent when the fumes of the repast met the nostrils of those destined to swallow it."

And yet the Lowood portion of Jane Eyre is gripping, pathetic, forceful—greater than the sum of its parts when these are considered in isolation. What animates the formal language? Drives homes the circumlocution? Herbert Read provides an answer, which, although general and impressionistic, is nonetheless telling: he speaks of a kind of prose which is written in a "mood of compulsion" generated from a "state of internal necessity." [11] This is well said, and describes what must have

11. Herbert Read, *English Prose Style* (New York, 1928), p. 110.

been the animating force behind the creation of Charlotte
Brontë's fiction.[12] However, this "internal necessity" found its
outlet in certain forms, clothed itself in certain idiosyncracies
of style, so that on the formal level one can point to various
stylistic devices and say *this* creates animation or *that* provides
drama. Thus, the animation of Brontë's prose can be traced to
those traits we have already found to be particularly characteristic of it: the stressed adverb, short clauses, syntactical inversion, balanced antitheses, figurative language, and a vocabulary
which, though formal in part, is also concrete, forceful, and
poetic.

Perhaps it is a mistake, however, to dichotomize Charlotte
Brontë's language too strictly, for the emotive and the formal
in her prose have this much in common: they are both rather
literary than conversational. And from what other source, considering her isolation, could the author have acquired her language? As in *Wuthering Heights*, there is no mean in Charlotte's
language between the dialect of local Yorkshire characters and
the formal poetic language of the narrator: these two extremes
were the closest to her experience.[13] The many literary allusions

12. It is interesting that several aspects of Charlotte Brontë's style cor-
respond to the stylistic characteristics of suicide notes—written, of course,
under extreme compulsion—as described by Charles E. Osgood in "Some
Effects of Motivation on the Style of Encoding," in *Style in Language*, ed.
Thomas A. Sebeok (Cambridge, Mass., 1960). For example, Brontë's
repetition of words corresponds to the greater stereotype of choice in
suicide notes; she uses, too, like the suicide notes, "allness" terms—
never, forever, always, no one—as I have endeavored to show in chapter
1; she uses frequent "mands"—utterances which express a subjective need
and require an answer from another person, usually cast in the imperative;
her attitudes are frequently "ambivalent evaluative assertions" that show
conflicting motives toward an attitude object ("I love you"; "you never
trusted me"; "I always quarreled with you"; "I stuck by our marriage
though"; for example). As I have tried to show, ambivalence is the key
to Brontë's themes and style: to cite just one novel, Lucy Snowe's feelings
for everyone are a mixture of respect, admiration, and contempt—even
for M. Paul Emanuel.

13. W. A. Craik discusses Charlotte Brontë's style only briefly, but very
sensibly points out that an author spending her formative years in the
West Riding of Yorkshire with an Irish father and a Cornish aunt, re-

in the novels alone testify to the importance and the reality literature possessed for the author. One remembers Robert Moore and Caroline Helstone reading *Coriolanus* aloud, perhaps, without realizing that the plot of the patrician Moore and the rabble mill hands *is* a version of Shakespeare's play. There is the scene where Caroline paces back and forth, reciting "The Castaway," a poem which inspires more than a dozen other allusions to shipwreck and drowning throughout the novel. There is Jane Eyre's apostrophe to the golden age of literature just past and to Scott's *Marmion*. There are the many, many allusions to *The Pilgrim's Progress* and the Bible. Shirley's ardent attack upon Milton's Eve is answered in her own *devoir*, which depicts the first woman, not like Milton, as a cook, but as a sublime creature in which genius and humanity are united. And the novels are thickly strewn with innumerable fragments of verse: Ginevra Fanshawe has a "bread-and-butter-eating, school-girl air"; when Adèle is told she cannot appear before the company, "some natural tears she shed"; and Jane opines that one must "burst" with boldness and good will into the "silent sea" of the stoic's soul.

While literary language and allusion indicate Charlotte Brontë's deep involvement with literature, they undoubtedly testify also to a certain self-consciousness in the author, a pride in learning, a desire to impress. Like Louis Moore, Charlotte Brontë is poor, therefore she must be proud. This perhaps explains also her use of the French language—in *The Professor* and *Villette* thickly (and naturally), in *Jane Eyre* and *Shirley* whenever the possibility arises. There was a trend, of course, stemming from the Romantic movement in literature and active in England and on the Continent, to create verisimilitude in the novel through the use of local dialects; but Charlotte Brontë belongs to this trend by virtue of her lively rendering of Yorkshire dialect rather than her French dialogue. In *Shirley*, a novel depending a good deal for its appeal on the salt of localisms, the French is often decidedly out of place; for example,

---

ceiving only intermittent education and regular writing training only in French, cannot be expected to write a standard southern English (*The Brontë Novels* [London, 1968], p. 194).

in the totally gratuitous remark concerning Mrs. Gale's irritation with the curates: " 'C'en est trop,' she would say, if she could speak French." Even Charlotte Brontë is aware of inappropriateness in *Shirley*, and is moved to apologize in parenthesis and footnote.

To recapitulate briefly. While sentences controlled by short clauses, heavy punctuation, and antithesis create a prose of syntactic restraint, Brontë's language, in contrast, is emotive, conflicting, and dramatic. This is so partly because Brontë's language is dominantly figurative, thus appealing to the imagination and the emotions rather than to the rational or objective. But figurative language per se does not account for the drama of the Brontë voice. The key lies in the fact that the metaphors cluster around thematic antitheses that dominate the novels. Because passion is not apt to be imaginatively expressed in the same terms as restraint, or plenty of terms of privation, conflict is created from the dynamic contrast between metaphors such as "a ridge of lighted heath, alive, glancing, devouring, would have been a meet emblem of my mind" and "the chill, icy hand of Reason"; between "food, sweet and strange, gathered amongst gleaning angels" and "the gnawed bone dogs had forsaken." But there are further contrasts within Brontë's language. The learned, formal language indicates on the one hand Brontë's consciousness of her learning, her literary heritage, her style, her public. The omnipresence of words like *mutinous, rebellious, overthrow, power*, and *revolt* mingling with verbs such as *shriek, shrill, rack, torture*, or *shatter*, however, express a violence and frustration that would seem to spring spontaneously from the deepest source of the author's being: the dichotomy is almost between the public and the private. The additional contrast between sentence structure and the language as a whole again confirms the conflict in the author's mind between the restrained and the effusive, the formal and the free. The result is a style that remains unsynthesized, but which ultimately draws its force from its immiscible and conflicting parts.

5

ARRAIGNED AT THE BAR
COURTROOM LANGUAGE
IN *JANE EYRE*

If divided in general about the merits of Charlotte Brontë's novels, readers can surely agree upon one characteristic of her fiction: its intensity. Narrowly plotted, myopically circumscribed, her novels still have the power to grip and to stir, a power usually arrogated by wide-screen human adventures like *War and Peace, Moby Dick,* or *King Lear.* From their plots, as David Cecil points out, we would expect Charlotte Brontë's novels to be as uneventful as *Northanger Abbey;* the impression they make, however, is more like that of *The Brothers Karamazov.*[1] Much of this intensity is generated thematically by the obsessive reiteration of a few motifs—loneliness, physical and mental suffering, moral righteousness, love—within a

1. David Cecil, *Victorian Novelists* (Chicago, 1958), p. 121. Cecil's evaluation of Charlotte Brontë, although unsympathetic at times, still seems to me essentially sound. The phrase "myopically circumscribed" is literally as well as figuratively true of the novels: Brontë characters often experience difficulty in "making out" a countenance or recognizing a face in the gloom (see, for example, *Shirley*, p. 195). While sometimes this visual difficulty is thematic or dramatic, often Brontë is undoubtedly recording her own experiences with poor eyesight.

close circle of action and event. Much of it is generated formally by the obsessive repetition of certain structural traits, as the foregoing discussion endeavored to prove. This obsessiveness, as we have seen, is not limited to syntactical structure, but extends, predictably, to Charlotte Brontë's language as well. Having examined the nature of Brontë's language in general, let us look more closely at the language of a particular novel, *Jane Eyre*.

Several of the more insistent patterns of imagery in *Jane Eyre* have received critical attention: the elemental (fire, ice); the natural (wind, moon, earthquake); the arboreal. As David Lodge aptly suggests, these "poetical flights" grow quite naturally out of the literal staples of the novels, so that Brontë's prose moves from the literal to the metaphorical with ease.[2] Hearth fire, seasonal change, the lushly flowering grounds of Thornfield—all actualities—become metaphorical means for describing passion, comfort, love; emotional fulfillment or deprivation; sexual frustration or fruition. This imagery is direct, uncomplicated, and often staggeringly intense.

Of a different cast is language, present in *Jane Eyre*, that can loosely be described as courtroom or legal terminology. This language differs from the more sporadic and deliberate imagery in its omnipresence: there is scarcely a page that does not contain some of these terms and hardly a chapter in which whole clusters of these words do not appear. It must, in fact, be emphasized from the beginning that the examples of legal terminology cited in this chapter comprise only a fraction of those words actually present in the novel. Chapter 27, for example, contains approximately one hundred of these words and phrases, only a few of which are mentioned below. This "presence factor" suggests that, unlike the imagery of nature and element, this courtroom language is often used unconsciously by Charlotte Brontë. This likelihood is furthered by the fact that, contrary to imagery patterns, this language rarely arises

2. David Lodge, *The Language of Fiction* (London, 1966), pp. 128–129. Lodge's essay "Fire and Eyre: The War of the Elements in *Jane Eyre*" has recently been reprinted in *The Brontës*, ed. Ian Gregor (Englewood Cliffs, N.J., 1970), pp. 110–136.

from the literal circumstances of the novel. Courtroom language would thus seem to have an even more subtle grip on Brontë's imagination than her more natural—and obvious—predilection for images of fire, moonlight, or ice; it seems probable, therefore, that this language may be profitably examined for the light it can cast on the meaning of *Jane Eyre*. Of equal interest: the fire, moonlight, and ice images come directly from the author's own environment and experience. But how did Charlotte Brontë's mind become steeped in the jargon of trial and courtroom—and, more significantly, why? Let us for the moment postpone this extra-fictional consideration, however.

Courtroom language exists in *Jane Eyre* on three different levels. On the first level it is literal, necessitated by the actual legal events in the novel. These are only two: the interruption of Jane and Rochester's marriage on the grounds of its illegality, and Jane's £20,000 inheritance, bequeathed to her by the Madeira uncle, John Eyre. In chapter 26, therefore, a great many legal terms appear in connection with plot circumstances: " 'My name is Briggs—*a solicitor* of — Street, London. . . . I would remind you of your lady's existence, sir; which *the law* recognizes, if you do not. . . . I have a *witness to the fact*; whose *testimony* even you, sir, will scarcely *controvert*' " (pp. 275–276). *Jane Eyre* is not, however, a novel in which legal transgression and its punishment by law is a major concern—as it is, for example, in Fielding's *Amelia* and *Jonathan Wild*, in *A Tale of Two Cities, Great Expectations, Bleak House,* and *Little Dorrit,* in *Crime and Punishment* or *Les Misérables.* Rochester's attempted bigamy, a central moral issue, does not involve legal process since it remains undiscovered until the day of the wedding and is prevented in a matter of minutes. All the more interesting, therefore, is Charlotte Brontë's insistent casting of event into the lexical framework of courtroom, trial, and conviction.

The second level of language comprises those terms which, because of the way they cluster and because of the figurative resemblance of the scenes they describe to courtroom procedure, have almost certainly been used deliberately by the author. Sometimes they occur metaphorically, as when, for example, Brontë says of Adèle that she is *"grave as any judge,"* or describes Grace Poole "companionless as *a prisoner in his dungeon."* Many of the terms are used literally in phrases like "I *judged him innocent,"* so that rather than the words, it is the situation which is figuratively "courtroom" here. The situations vary, however, in the degree to which they are figurative. When Jane ponders the culpability of Grace Poole, for example, we are very near to literal crime:

> [I was] occupied in puzzling my brains over the enigmatical character of Grace Poole . . . in *questioning* why she had not been *given into custody* . . . . He [Rochester] had almost as much as declared his *conviction* of her *criminality* last night: what mysterious *cause* withheld him from *accusing* her . . . that even when she lifted her hand against his life, he dared not openly *charge her with the attempt,* much less *punish* her for it. (pp. 148–149)

Most of the time, however, the language describes situations only figuratively related to actual legal infraction: an instance is St. John's behavior after Jane has refused to marry him: ". . . he made me feel what *severe punishment,* a good, yet stern, a conscientious, yet implacable man can *inflict* on one who has *offended* him . . . he contrived to *impress* me momently with the *conviction* that I was put *beyond the pale* of his favour" (pp. 389–390). Let us call this stratum of courtroom or legal phraseology the conscious level.

Finally, there is the language which occurs simply in the natural course of narration where it has ostensibly nothing to do with either figurative or literal legal process at all. When Charlotte Brontë writes, "He *summoned* me to his presence," of "the *inmates* of Thornfield," we would not, under ordinary circumstances, seize upon these words as conspicuously legal even though *summons* and *inmate* belong to the lexicon of trial and punishment. But, of course, these are not ordinary circumstances: the language of fiction is largely deliberate; in any situation where choice is possible, therefore, word selection is significant. Brontë might have written, after all, "He *sent for* me," or have called the *inmates, residents*. I do not mean to insist too strenuously on the importance of this stratum, yet it seems useful to note its presence. This stratum of terminology can be termed the unconscious level. Incidentally, the question of whether or not Charlotte Brontë was familiar with all these as legal terms arises, but must be dismissed as impossible to answer, and, basically, irrelevant; the words are there.[3]

II

Since the novel falls naturally by location and event into five parts, let us examine this motif of courtroom and trial according to these divisions. Discussion will be chiefly concerned with clusters of terms on what has been labeled the conscious level, only a fraction of which can be dealt with.

In the first parts of the novel, dealing with Jane's childhood at Gateshead and Lowood, events coincide most closely to actual courtroom trial: the child Jane is convicted by adults of "criminal" behavior and is sentenced to punishment on three separate occasions. These episodes are well-known and straightforward, and there is no need to describe them other than to call attention to how the text is infused with trial and punishment terms. In the first instance, Jane has come to actual physical blows with her mortal foe, John Reed. Having told the reader how John *punishes* her and how she has no *appeal* against his *inflictions*, she calls him a *murderer*, and is dragged away by Abbot and Bessie to the red-room as punishment. There, "conscious that a moment's mutiny had already rendered [her] *liable* to strange *penalties*," she is thrust upon a stool, *arrested* by two pair of hands, and watches a "preparation for *bonds*" (pp. 10–12). The famous red-room episode follows wherein Jane wrestles with resentment, then guilt, and finally, terror. Her situation is very deliberately rendered in terms of

3. Words I have denoted as "legal" or belonging to the lexicon of trial and courtroom are confirmed by the *Oxford English Dictionary* as in use in law before or during the composition of *Jane Eyre*.

crime and punishment, for her child's mind has magnified the event to this proportion. Jane tries the lock and finds that "no *jail* was ever more *secure*"; she questions furiously *why* she is "always *accused,* for ever *condemned*"; compares her persecution to the unjust partiality shown to Georgiana who can "purchase *indemnity* for every *fault,*" to John who is never *punished,* while she dares *commit* no *fault.* Her frenzy mounts, she is beseiged by guilt: she has been thinking of starving herself—"that certainly was a *crime.*" She remembers spirits who return to *punish the perjured;* she imagines in a moment of climactic terror that she is indeed being visited by the ghost of Mr. Reed. A fit follows; the household is roused; she begs her aunt to be *punished* in some other way, but Mrs. Reed is adamant and Jane is *locked in* "without further parley" (pp. 14–18).

For her second trial, Jane, who in the meantime has been *condemned* to the nursery, is ordered into the presence of Mr. Brocklehurst and Mrs. Reed. The scene is, in effect, a cross-examination of the suspect by the judge rather than a prosecuting attorney. Jane *deliberates,* gives honest rather than exonerating answers, and Mr. Brocklehurst pronounces that her defense *proves* she has a wicked heart. Mrs. Reed, witness for the prosecution, confirms Jane's wickedness, and Jane stands condemned, shedding tears, "the impotent *evidences*" of her anguish (pp. 32–33).

The punishment threatened by Brocklehurst at Gateshead becomes reality at Lowood. In the schoolroom Jane drops her slate, Brocklehurst's eye falls upon her, and she is summoned before *the dread judge.* The episode (pp. 63–65) occasions a spate of courtroom language on both the conscious and unconscious levels: *charged with, enchained, elude, escaped, notice, conceal, counsel, punished, conviction, marked character, case, sustained, trial, punish, weigh, kneel before, my judge,* etc. Present also are such standard phrases as, " 'Let the child who broke her slate come forward,' " " 'It becomes my duty to warn you,' " and the reading of the sentence: " 'Let her stand half an hour longer on that stool, and let no one speak to her during the remainder of the day.' " This schoolroom humiliation comes closest in the book to an actual trial; it *is* an unofficial trial.

It will be readily remembered that Jane is not the only victim of punishment at Lowood: Helen Burns undergoes continual chastisement at the hands of Miss Scatcherd with a meekness that is meant, of course, to thematically complement Jane's fierce resentment. Jane, normally, resents accusation and punishment, and cannot rest content until cleared of false imputation in the eyes of the whole school. The issue is resolved, again in courtroom language: Miss Temple agrees first that "when a *criminal* is *accused*, he is always *allowed to speak in his own defense*. You have been *charged with falsehood*; *defend* yourself to me as well as you can" (p. 69). Jane does, with the result that: "Miss Temple, having assembled the whole school, announced that *inquiry had been made into the charges alleged against* Jane Eyre, and that she was most happy to be able *to pronounce her completely cleared from every imputation*. The teachers then shook hands with me and kissed me, and a murmur of pleasure ran through the ranks of my companions" (p. 72). Jane's character is thus more firmly approved than ever, and the Lowood section ends in the triumph of the obscure orphan over circumstance and the desire for a new proving ground. Near-literal circumstances of trial have firmly established the motif of crime and punishment which is to appear in a more subtle—and therefore more interesting—form throughout the rest of the novel.

At Thornfield, Jane is briefly stirred by the news that there is an absent master, described by Mrs. Fairfax as *just* and *unimpeachable*, but soon grows weary of the very security she had longed for and chafes against her bonds: "Who *blames* me? . . . Millions are *condemned* to a stiller *doom* than mine . . . . It is thoughtless to *condemn* them . . ." (pp. 105–106). She is almost immediately rescued from boredom, however, for a cloaked horseman appears on the scene and invokes her aid. The flurry of legal language used to describe the fallen-horse episode—*summon, obey, injured, swearing, pronouncing, try, officious, extorted, stand questioning, will*—most of it on the unconscious level, foreshadows Rochester's second appearance in the novel. For this he is cast, as both action and language clearly show, in the role of a judge, and Jane is on trial again:

Unused as I was to strangers, it was rather *a trial* to *appear*
thus formally *summoned* in Mr. Rochester's presence. . . .
"*Let Miss Eyre be seated,*" said he . . . . "Miss Eyre, you are
not so unsophisticated as Adèle: she demands a 'cadeau,' clam-
ourously, the moment she sees me: you beat about the bush."
"Because I have less confidence in my *desserts* than Adèle
has: she can *prefer the claim* of old acquaintance, and the *right*
too of custom . . . but if I had *to make out a case* I should be
puzzled . . . ."
"Oh, don't fall back on over-modesty! I have *examined*
Adèle . . . ." (pp. 115–117)

and later:

"Don't trouble yourself *to give her a character,*" returned
Mr. Rochester: "eulogiums will not *bias* me; I shall *judge* for
myself. . . ."
". . . I should hardly have been able to guess your age. It is
a point difficult to fix where the features and countenance are
so much at variance as *in your case.*" (pp. 118–119)

Jane is ordered to "*produce evidence*":

"Well, fetch me your portfolio, if you can *vouch* for its contents being original; but don't *pass your word* unless you are
certain: I can *recognize* patchwork."
"Then I will say nothing, and you shall *judge* for yourself,
sir. . . ."
. . . when he had *examined* them . . . "*resume your seat, and
answer my questions.*" (p. 120)

Jane's responses this time win favor, the "grim" and "stern"
judge is won, and it soon falls out—with psychological truth—
that the high-handed judge is himself obsessed with guilt and
wishes to confess and be judged by one who has proven to be
of clear conscience:

"I have plenty of *faults* . . . I don't wish to *palliate* them . . . .
I have a past existence, a series of *deeds* . . . which might well
call my sneers and *censures* from my neighbors to myself . .

like other *defaulters*, I like to *lay* half *the blame* on ill fortune and adverse *circumstances* . . . . I envy you your peace of mind, your *clean conscience* . . . ." (p. 130)

Encouraged by Jane's honesty and innocence, Rochester swears to reform: "I know what my aim is, what my *motives* are; and at this moment I *pass a law* . . . that both are *right*" (p. 132). Here begins the theme of Rochester's guilt and trial which ends only with his punishment and atonement at the conclusion of the novel. Jane, who at the beginning of their relationship was herself "on trial," becomes Rochester's judge and will listen throughout her stay at Thornfield to Rochester's confessions—first about Céline, then about Mason, and finally about his marriage to Bertha Mason. As at Lowood, Jane is not only proven innocent, but morally and intellectually superior to those about her.

And yet, if Jane has been judged honest and unstained by Rochester, she is well aware of her own weaknesses, and is her own severest judge. Already passionately in love with her master, his thrilling "My cherished preserver, good-night," still ringing in her ears, she is brought up sharply the very next morning after the fire by the news of his sudden departure for the estate of Blanche Ingram, described by Mrs. Fairfax with unconscious cruelty as ravishingly desirable. There follows the well-known metaphorical trial scene in which Jane *"reviews the information*, looks into her heart, *examines* its thoughts and feeling":

> *Arraigned at my own bar, Memory having given her evidence . . . Reason having come forward and told in her own quiet way, a plain, unvarnished tale . . . I pronounced judgment to this effect:—*
> That a greater fool than Jane Eyre had never breathed the breath of life: that a more fantastic idiot had never surfeited herself on sweet *lies*, and swallowed poison as if it were nectar. . . . *"Listen, then, Jane Eyre, to your sentence* . . . ." (pp. 152–153)

Jane condemns herself to the punishment of making and contemplating two portraits—one of the georgeous Blanche, one of herself. But Rochester returns, and reason is inevitably thrust back into the darkest cell.

The house-party chapters are particularly interesting in that the language of the courtroom appears heavily in a situation that is only very obliquely a trial. Jane is summoned as usual to appear in the drawing room by Mr. Rochester, who states that if she *resists*, he will fetch her in *case of contumacy*; she, however, *pleads off* and he *admits her plea* (p. 161). He is insistent upon the next occasion and she is forced to appear; he enters, and she admits that, although Rochester is "not beautiful, *according to rule*," he is beautiful to her; that her feelings are taken from her own power and *fettered* in his (p. 166). Here Blanche becomes the center of interest and usurps the language of courtroom: governesses are being discussed and she moves " 'introduction of a new topic,' " begging Rochester to " 'second [her] motion' " (p. 169). Then, commanding him to sing a Corsair song, she admonishes: " 'Gardez-vous en bien! If you *err* willfully, I shall *devise a proportionate punishment*.' " Rochester, picking up the metaphor, replies that she must be *clement*, that she has the power of *chastisement* beyond mortal endurance, and that one of her frowns would be " 'a sufficient substitute for *capital punishment*' " (p. 171). The episode culminates in a game of charades in which the subject chosen by Rochester's group, *Bridewell*, further enforces the culpability theme. All this time, from her corner, Jane has been *witnessing* and *judging*, first *condemning* Rochester and then deciding that she does not feel "*justified* in *judging* and *blaming* either him or Miss Ingram" (p. 178). Thus a scene which has often been decreed blatantly awkward is subtly laced with the theme of trial: Jane is judged inferior by the guests; Rochester is trying her emotional fidelity and, at the same time, Blanche's temperament; Blanche is testing her powers over Rochester; and throughout Jane is judging guests, Blanche, and above all, Rochester, whom she suspects of desiring to marry for crass interest.

The subsequent fortune-telling scene in which Jane is examined by Rochester is so obvious an instance again of Jane-on-trial that we may pass it over, only noting the rash of legal language with which it is depicted: *detect, warrant, chastise, meted, deny, charge, claims, counsel, swear*—the reader may complete the list for himself. Let us leap ahead to the moment when, the fearful night of horror past, Rochester is compelled by the evidence Jane has seen while tending Mason and by his own crushing guilt and despair *to put a case* to Jane (pp. 206–207). Admitting he has committed a *capital error*, but distinguishing between *crime*—the "'shedding of blood or any other guilty act*, which might make the *perpetrator amenable to the law*'"—and *error*, he asks Jane whether, to lead a better life, one is "'*justified* in over-leaping an obstacle of custom—a mere conventional impediment, which neither your *conscience* sanctifies nor your *judgment approves?*'" And again, "'Is the wandering and *sinful*, but now rest-seeking and *repentant*, man *justified* in daring the world's opinion . . . ?'" To which Jane replies that men and women are *fallible*; that man must "'look higher than his equals for strength *to amend*, and solace to heal.'"

The scene is important for several reasons. Since the piety of Helen Burns—rejected by Jane—this is the first time the novel moves significantly from the secular to the divine level of judgment; it is the first time the word *crime* has been adjusted to the word *sin*. All the "trials" in the novel so far have been human, social; all the punishment man-inflicted. Jane's response at this point is feeble because it does not tally with her experience, which has shown that far from being helpless, man has a conscience, a will, and a reason which can guide him through a precarious existence. In mouthing conventionalities about looking Above for solace, she belies her own nature—fiercely desirous of human sympathy and approval. And her response does Rochester no good at all, for he decides to seek solace in committing bigamy instead.

In the interim before Rochester's proposal, the discovery and flight, Jane is recalled to Gateshead to salve the conscience of her dying aunt. Mrs. Reed, arraigned at her own bar, confesses her guilt, dramatically reversing roles with Jane who had once "a hundred times been *sentenced to kneel, to ask pardon for offenses*, by me, *uncommitted*" (p. 218). On her return to

Thornfield she is greeted by Rochester—" *'Truant, truant'* "—
and the chestnut-tree scene follows apace. This episode (chap.
23), not surprisingly, is studded with courtroom language,
much of which comprises words of oath-taking and swearing;
it culminates in Rochester's words: " 'Jane, I *summon* you as
my wife.' " Mingling with the legal terminology are words connotative of divine law: " 'It will *atone* . . . . It will *expiate* at
God's *tribunal*. I know my Maker *sanctions* what I do. For the
world's *judgment*—I wash my hands thereof. For man's opinion—I *defy* it' " (p. 243). The words are deeply ironic, for in
the event, man's opinion—the world's judgment—prevents the
longed-for marriage, and his Maker, far from sanctioning his
behavior, strikes him blind and crippled.

Between the proposal of marriage and the day of the thwarted wedding, Jane, it will be remembered, cools Rochester's heat
by a great deal of teasing asperity, and much of this lovers'
banter is cast in legal terminology. Jane, for example, questions
the duration of Rochester's affection:

> "I wonder how you will answer me a year hence, should I ask
> a favour it does not *suit* your convenience or pleasure to *grant*."
> "Ask me something now, Janet . . . ."
> "Indeed, I will, sir; I have my *petition* all ready. . . ."
> "What? what? . . . Curiosity is a dangerous *petition*: it is well
> I have not *taken a vow* to accord every request—" (p. 248)

And later, Jane's railing at Rochester's "Turkish tastes" employs
metaphors of bonds and legal documents:

> ". . . you . . . sir, shall in a trice find yourself *fettered* amongst
> our hands: nor will I, for one, consent to *cut your bonds* till
> you have *signed a charter* . . . I would *have no mercy*, Mr.
> Rochester, if you *supplicated* for it with an eye like that. While
> you looked so, I should be certain that whatever *charter* you
> might *grant under coercion*, your first *act*, when *released*, would
> be to *violate* its *conditions*."
> "Why, Jane . . . . You will *stipulate*, I see, for peculiar *terms*
> . . . ." (pp. 255–256)

This happy word-play, this mock drama of judge and witness which Jane and Rochester, as we have seen, enact from the beginning, receives a terrible check, when, on the day of the wedding, the realm of law suddenly becomes a reality and the ugly crime of bigamy is laid at Rochester's door. As noted above, the language of law is here coldly literal; it becomes metaphorical again as Rochester is put through the painful confession of his nightmare marriage (chap. 27). The question of guilt, however, does not involve Rochester alone. A more subtle issue is at stake when an alternative to bigamy—adultery —is offered to Jane. Is not Jane equally at fault, *more* at fault, for refusing to live with the man she loves?

> "And what a distortion in your *judgment*, what a perversity in your ideas, is *proved* by your conduct! Is it better to drive a fellow-creature to despair than to *transgress* a mere *human law* —no man being *injured by the breach?* . . ."
>
> This was true: and while he spoke my very *conscience* and reason *turned traitors* against me, and *charged* me with *crime* in *resisting* him. (pp. 300–301)

Jane decides to "'*keep the law* given by God,'" less, however, from piety than from pride, for Rochester's confessions of past dissipation have left her firmly convinced of one thing: should she yield to him physically, she would only lose his esteem. Since esteem is lifeblood to Jane Eyre, its loss would be insupportable: "I did not give utterance to this *conviction* . . . . I impressed it on my heart, that it might remain there to *serve* me as aid in the time of *trial*" (p. 296). Rochester is made aware of the impossibility of winning her by physical force: here language of prison and escape becomes an Elizabethan-like metaphor for body and spirit: "'If I tear, if I rend the slight *prison*, my outrage will only *let the captive loose*. Conqueror I might be of the house; but the *inmate* would *escape* to heaven . . .'" (p. 302). Jane, unviolated, makes her escape, comparing her blind misery at leaving Rochester to a prisoner's, who, "taken out to pass through a fair scene to the *scaffold*," has lost all interest in the world's loveliness in contemplating the horrors of death; and the Thornfield chapter of her life ends. Courtroom language, thickly studded throughout the first two-thirds of the novel, now tapers off slightly. This is appropriate, for the protagonist has passed through her greatest trial, and, though emotionally scathed, is free from the emotional and legal fetters of an adulterous passion. Yet, in Jane's first interview with the people who have befriended her, she is again on the witness stand (indeed, she has been accused of housebreaking by the servant Hannah). St. John Rivers, with folded arms, and eyes "that *search* other people's thoughts," appears to Jane as *"this penetrating young judge."* After admitting that the Rivers family has a *claim* on her gratitude, Jane (under an *alias*) tells the trio a bit of her history, insisting that in leaving her position as governess she was guiltless: " 'No *blame attached* to me: I am as *free from culpability* as any one of you three' " (p. 329). And, as in the past, Jane not only convinces her judges of her integrity, but eventually, because of her puritan honesty, conscientiousness, and diligence, subtly claims, and is granted, the right to judge others, even the man of God, St. John.

When St. John is not described in metaphor of ice and marble, he is frequently depicted in legal language. Sometimes he is a prisoner, one who *"locks* every feeling and pang within— expresses, *confesses*, imparts nothing." More often he is a jailor who *"holds* Jane *in thrall,"* whose kiss is like *"a seal affixed to [her] fetters,"* whose praise "is more *restraining* than his indifference" (pp. 377–378). Frequently he is the prosecuting attorney, as, for example, when he detects Jane's identity: " 'I *confess* I had my *suspicions*, but it was only yesterday afternoon they were at once *resolved into certainty*. You *own* the name and renounce the ALIAS? . . . You must *prove your identity*, of course . . . if you had *committed a murder*, and I had told you your *crime was discovered*, you could scarcely look more aghast' " (pp. 362–363).

All these roles merge in St. John's grim battle to enlist Jane in the missionary work with which he is obsessed. She is particularly vulnerable to his urging, of course, because she is unconsciously tormented with guilt for deserting Rochester.

This battle is related largely in legal language: Rivers *claims* Jane, he *summons* her, but Jane initially feels no response: her mind is *"like a rayless dungeon, with one shrinking fear fettered in its depths . . ."* (p. 382–383). Yet she wavers, for to lose her cousin's friendship would *try* her severely. Rivers asserts that Jane *merits severe reproof* for her *offense* in refusing his offer; he *proves* her absurdity in rejecting him; she insists there is no *" 'breach of promise,* no desertion *in the case.' "* Rivers calls her interest in Rochester *lawless*; she *confesses* her still vivid interest in him (pp. 392–393). The battle culminates in Jane's near-capitulation; however, in the very throes of indecision, just when St. John has laid his hand upon her head as if to *claim* her, Jane is *summoned* by another appeal, the voice of Edward Fairfax Rochester. She thus escapes a relationship which she has admitted would not only enslave her, but would torture and even kill her.

At the Rochester Arms, Jane hears of her master's fate from the innkeeper who has *witnessed* the tragedy and rejected (as the reader must) the opinion that it was *just judgment* upon the owner of Thornfield (p. 407). Jane flies to Ferndean: there she finds the blind Rochester like "some *wronged* and *fettered* wild beast or bird, dangerous to approach in his sullen woe." She does approach him and there is a sudden flurry of legal metaphor: "He groped; I *arrested* his wandering hand, and *prisoned* it in both mine. . . . The muscular hand *broke from my custody*; my arm was *seized* . . . the *conviction* of the reality of all this *seized* him" (p. 412). The hour of reunion over, Jane is soon on the stand again: she has told Rochester of Rivers and he responds with, *" 'you will be pleased just to answer me a question or two,' "* whereupon, "Then followed this *cross-examination"* (p. 419). Jealousy is dispelled, love redeclared, and the resolution to marry taken: *" 'Jane suits me: do I suit her?' 'To the finest fibre of my nature, sir.' 'The case being so . . .* we must be married instantly' "* (p. 423).

The secular climax of the novel past, there remains but Rochester's confession of pride and repentance. Here, as in the scene of Rochester's original proposal, the language of secular law merges with the language of divine law while a distinction is drawn between the two: God "'*judges* not as man *judges*, but far more wisely. I *did wrong*: I would have sullied my innocent flower—breathed *guilt* on its purity: the Omnipotent snatched it from me. . . . HIS *chastisements* are mighty . . .'" (p. 424). And Rochester prays, because "'in the midst of *judgment* [God] has remembered *mercy.*'" The "irreligious dog" has become pious, convinced both by Jane's condemnation of his behavior in her role of judge and by the horror of his punishment, that he is indeed a sinner. The trial over, the prisoner's sentence mitigated, it is not surprising that the last chapter of the novel, which describes Jane and Rochester's married bliss, contains virtually no courtroom language on any of the three levels: the drama of guilt, crime, and punishment, which has enmeshed almost every character in the novel, is played out.

III

Awareness of this all-pervading legal language in the very bloodstream of the novel must certainly reinforce some interpretations of *Jane Eyre*, while weakening others. Its presence, for example, considerably weakens the claim that Charlotte Brontë's novel is a wild tale of romance played out in a never-never land of wicked stepmothers and Gothic dungeons: few realms are more everyday, more sober, more socially realistic than the arena where the machinery of secular law inexorably grinds. The financial terms that pepper Jane Austen's novels and give them such a mundane tone have been noted;[4] the legal terminology in *Jane Eyre* has some of the same effect. While it is true that some of the words have a romantic rather than a realistic aura—*fetters, dungeon, captive*—and that some of the "legal" situations are dramatically figurative, most of the terms are unevocative legal jargon. Once noted, their presence, I believe, indicates that the central action of the novel is bound more firmly to the real world than has often been supposed.

4. Dorothy Van Ghent, "On Pride and Prejudice," *The English Novel: Form and Function* (New York, 1953), pp. 99–111.

This fictional world is not the simple realm of the fairy tale or the romance where a kind of crude justice holds sway, but the complex world of the human conscience which must *scrutinize, suspect, conjecture, weigh, affirm, examine,* and *judge.* In the melodramatic destruction of Thornfield and the near-destruction of its master, there is indeed an attempt to simplify a complex moral issue of crime and punishment, although Rochester's punishment has less to it of romance and fairy tale than of the Bible, where terrible and often incomprehensible chastisement is meted out by an avenging God. This simplification, however, belies the complex theme of conscience and human judgment embodied in the very lexical tissues of the novel.

Another interpretation that this legal language calls into question is the claim that *Jane Eyre* is chiefly a Christian parable, a novel that has for its theme the workings of God's providence, or even a predominantly religious novel.[5] Certainly there is a distinction drawn clearly in the book between two levels of law and justice—human and divine. It is significant, for instance, that Rochester brings both a lawyer and a clergyman to the scene of the maniac's confinement: he seeks acquittal from each. Certainly Rochester's testimony that "God judges not as man judges, but far more wisely," gives weight to the Divine providence theme, coming as it does at the end (not the climax) of the novel.

But the presence throughout of considerably more terms from

5. See, for example, Barbara Hardy, *The Appropriate Form* (London, 1964), pp. 61–62; Frederick Flahiff, "Formative Ideas in the Novels of Charlotte and Emily Brontë," *DA,* vol. 27, 746–747A (Toronto); Robert Martin, *The Accents of Persuasion* (London, 1966): "*Jane Eyre* is at bottom . . . largely a religious novel, concerned with the meaning of religion to man and its relevance to his behavior" (p. 81); Joseph Prescott, "*Jane Eyre:* A Romantic Exemplum with a Difference," in *Twelve Original Essays on Great English Novels,* ed. Charles Shapiro (Detroit, 1960), pp. 87–102. Kathleen Tillotson makes this evaluation: "This is not to counter the attack in the *Quarterly Review* by claiming *Jane Eyre* as a Christian novel; though it expresses, more directly than any other novel, the convictions of many creedless Christians in the eighteen-forties; the conviction that 'not a May-game is this man's life, but a battle and a march, a warfare with principalities and powers'" (*Novels of the Eighteen-Forties* [Oxford, 1954], p. 309).

secular rather than from religious law indicates instead that
Jane Eyre is principally a novel about man's capacity for judgment.[6] The crucial moments of the novel—Jane's decision to
leave Thornfield and her decision to reject St. John Rivers—
are expressed in language which emphatically stresses the author's central concern with the individual's conscience and his
ability to judge right from wrong: "To have yielded then [to
Rochester] would have been an *error of principle*; to have
yielded now would have been an *error of judgment*." Throughout the novel the emphasis has been on Jane's judgment: over
and over occurs the phrase "*I* deem": "*I* deem myself worthy,"
"*I* deem these right plans," "*I* deem it useless." Whatever else
may influence a reader to consider this a novel about God's
providence, the language of law, rooted in the secular processes
by which man's punishment and reward is meted out here on
earth, urges that this is a work of fiction concerned primarily
with self-judgment and self-control.

Finally, the courtroom language reinforces the interpretation
of *Jane Eyre* as a novel essentially radical in its preoccupation
with the themes of independence and liberty for the subju-
gated sex, Victorian woman. While the novel may end, as some
critics claim, in a domesticity that is hardly radical (although
as Rochester's moral and physical superior, possessed of an
independent income, Jane hardly occupies the position of the
ordinary Victorian wife), the language of the novel belies com-
placency or compromise. It does so particularly in the lexical
area referring to punishment, for punishment in *Jane Eyre* is
always to be in some way imprisoned. Sometimes this imprisonment takes the form of social exile: Jane among the Reeds, Jane
at the edges of the Thornfield house party, Jane wandering
through the village of Morton. More frequently the exile is
mental, for it is only with Rochester and Diana and Mary Rivers

6. The words *sin* and *wicked*, for example, occur much less frequently
than the secular *crime* and *criminal*. At the height of urging her Christian
doctrine, Helen Burns uses strongly secular terms: " 'Besides, with this
creed, I can so clearly distinguish between the *criminal* and his *crime*
. . .' " (*JE*, p. 57). St. John, in describing his mission, uses words like
advocate, swear, circumstance, claim, summons, case.

that Jane can find total sympathy. Often it is to be in fetters, enslaved: this is the key issue in her struggle with both Rochester and St. John, for one offers what Jane considers physical enslavement and degradation, the other mental enslavement. At other times, Jane's suffering arises from being prisoned by "the viewless fetters of an uniform and too still existence"—her sojourn at Lowood, or the first three deadly calm months at Thornfield. Her preoccupation with imprisonment is so strong that in dreams she visions herself barred, enclosed by darkness, burdened, fettered and unable to move:

> "On sleeping . . . I continued also the wish to be with you, and experienced a strange, regretful consciousness, of some barrier dividing us. During all my first sleep, I was following the windings of an unknown road; total obscurity environed me . . . I was burdened with the charge of a little child . . . . I thought, sir, that you were on the road a long way before me; and I strained every nerve to overtake you . . . but my movements were fettered; and my voice still died away inarticulate; while you, I felt, withdrew farther and farther every moment." (p. 267)

One reaction is aroused by Jane's frustration with these emotional and moral dungeons: an ardent desire for rebellion, for a breaking of bonds. Present therefore is a great deal of courtroom language which involves the condemned man's chafing against his confinement—the language of liberty, or (it is often the same thing) of independence. Jane first experiences the heady feeling of freedom after she has railed at Mrs. Reed: "It seemed as if an *invisible bond had burst*, and that I had struggled out into unhoped-for *liberty*" (p. 36). Her intense desire for freedom culminates in her cry to Rochester: " 'I am no bird; and no *net ensnares me*; I am a *free human being with an independent will*; which I now exert to leave you.' Another effort *set me at liberty*, and I stood erect before him" (p. 241).

The bird metaphor in the above quotation provides an appropriate place to observe that the theme of liberty is not borne exclusively by this legal lexicon, but is present in other areas of language, both literal and figurative, perhaps most strikingly in the many metaphoric references to birds. The following examples are typical; there are others:

> "I see at intervals the glance of a curious sort of bird through the close-set bars of a cage: a vivid, restless, resolute captive is there; were it but free, it would soar cloud-high." (p. 133)

> "Of yourself, you could come with soft flight and nestle against my heart, if you would: seized against your will you will elude the grasp like an essence...." (p. 302)

> ... a sad heart ... impotent as a bird with both wings broken, it still quivered its shattered pinions in vain attempts to seek him. (p. 307)

> ". . . my cramped existence all at once spread out to a plain without bounds—my powers heard a call from heaven to rise, gather their full strength, spread their wings, and mount beyond ken." (p. 343)

There is nothing original in equating freedom with the flight of a bird, yet this is striking language. Brontë's figurative language gains its force from the antagonism of its parts: against every expression of freedom—*bird, soar, elude, rise, spread their wings, mount*—is counterposed the language of restraint —*bars, cage, captive, grasp, wings broken, cramped existence*. This conflict exists on all levels of the novel; opposed to the language of freedom, supporting the many legal words connoting captivity, for example, are words denoting actual objects of confinement: the novel abounds in gates, fences, walls, narrow passages, low ceilings, cramped stairways, "apertures," latched windows, drawn blinds, locks, drawn bolts, and doors that are described, not as open, but as *unclosed*, suggesting in the author a morbid fascination with confinement as well as a horror of it. The buildings thus described are raised to the level of symbolic prisons: Gateshead is such; Lowood, "surrounded by walls so high as to exclude every glimpse of prospect" is another; Thornfield is literally for Bertha Rochester and figuratively for Rochester himself "this insolent vault."

Since there is no actual imprisonment, no real chains binding

Jane Eyre, this recurring language of imprisonment, punishment, escape, and freedom is a measure both of the depths of
the moral, intellectual, and spiritual dungeons to which Victorian society has condemned Jane Eyre and of the intensity
of the protagonist's desire to escape them. Few classes have
suffered such frustrating restrictions as the one to which Jane
Eyre belongs—a class educated to sympathize with the values
of the upper classes but denied the income and birth to realize
them. This theme of liberty is, of course, a corollary of the
theme of human judgment, since for Brontë personal freedom
can be won through the exercise of right reason—and both are
fundamentally linked to the novel's realism. The legal language,
as we have seen, emphasizes in Charlotte Brontë's novel these
three qualities, which have often been minimized or denied.

I V

An extra-literary question hovers unanswered in the air. *Jane
Eyre*, as the reader is aware, has virtually nothing to do with
actual legal process. While it is quite natural to cast an episode
like Jane's public humiliation at Lowood in the language of a
courtroom trial, the legal terms that crop up continually in the
love talk of Jane and Rochester, in the Jane-St. John encoun-
ters, in the house-party section, in Jane's interior monologues
(which, in fact, permeate the entire novel), since they so seldom arise from the literal events of the book, can reasonably be
assumed to reflect the bent of Charlotte Brontë's mind instead.
As a parson's daughter, Brontë's consciousness of "Divine tri-
bunals" is understandable, inevitable. While the sources of her
considerable lexicon of secular legal terms are less obvious,
several possibilities present themselves. We know from Mrs.
Gaskell of Reverend Brontë's keen interest in both local and
national politics, with all their legal ramifications. We know of
the precocious interest of the Brontë children in all the news-
papers had to report of parliamentary debate, of their vivid
discussions of political events. We can speculate that two au-

thors Charlotte Brontë read with particular enthusiasm might well have contributed to stocking her mind and her vocabulary with legal language: Shakespeare, whose plays abound in law terms, and Scott, whose novels frequently deal with the workings of the law—not surprisingly, since Scott was himself a barrister and a sheriff. More interesting than how Charlotte Brontë acquired a courtroom vocabulary, however, is the problem of why in *Jane Eyre* this language preoccupied her to such an extent. I would like to suggest that the answer may well lie in the one word conspicuous by its absence in the novel—guilt.

One does not have to search far to unearth reasons for the presence of a strong guilt complex in the author of *Jane Eyre*: they are patent in her career as a writer, and in the novel, as well as in her life. Every Brontë scholar is familiar with the young Charlotte's struggle to give up the passionate and turbid world of Angria and with her farewell to that world written at Roe Head in 1839: "I long to quit for awhile that burning clime where we have sojourned too long—its skies flame—the glow of sunset is always upon it—the mind would cease from excitement and turn now to a cooler region where the dawn breaks grey and sober, and the coming day for a time at least is subdued by clouds."[7]

Writing her first adult novel, *The Professor*, Charlotte Brontë indeed quit the burning clime of Angria: so consciously and effectively is all emotion suppressed that her heroine, Frances Henri, impresses one as little more than a pensive shadow, while the protagonist Crimsworth emerges from the controlled and rigid narrative a feelingless stick. After such a violent departure from Angria, a counter-stroke of the pendulum was inevitable. We can guess with what relief, and yet with what trepidation and inner conflict Brontë returned in *Jane Eyre* to a mode of expression so much more congenial to her nature— the frank narration of vivid feeling and action. Jane's occasional pious moralizing, almost as foreign to the spirit of the

7. T. J. Wise and J. A. Symington, eds., *The Miscellaneous and Unpublished Writings of Charlotte and Patrick Branwell Brontë*, vol. 2 (Oxford, 1936–1938), pp. 403–404.

novel as the passages of Christian didacticism to the pagan
Beowulf, may well be interpreted, I believe, as the restraints
imposed by an author who is acutely conscious that she is reverting to a type of writing she had deliberately abandoned
with the Angrian tales.

But, of course, it is not only the mode of expression of *Jane
Eyre* that may well have troubled its author, but the novel's
subject matter as well. We have already noted that the courtroom language in the novel indicates a preoccupation with
human rather than divine judgment, with individual rather
than institutionalized morality and religion. We have suggested
too that the courtroom terminology dealing with imprisonment
and escape reflects in the author a fierce desire for spiritual,
intellectual, and economic independence. Added to this is the
fact that *Jane Eyre* is an explosively passionate book which
describes its heroine's physical desire in exceptionally frank
terms. The whole novel, in fact, abounds in imagery of eroticism, conception, and pregnancy—the latter, as one critic has
observed, making it so evident that *Jane Eyre* was written by
a woman that Victorians must have been blind not to have tum-
bled immediately to the fact.[8] Jane seldom imagines anything:
she always *conceives* it. She is constantly *swelling* with joy,
expanding with life, quickening with emotion. Some of the
eroticism has been noted, particularly that occurring in the
Ferndean reunion chapter, but, of course, it is everywhere,
reaching almost comic proportions for the modern reader because of its obviousness in the passage in which St. John Rivers
describes himself as yielding, melting, overflowing with sweet
inundation, deluged with a nectarous flood.

These predilections—a preoccupation with physical love, a
rebellious desire for independence, a rooted belief in personal
rather than Divine guidance—all natural or praiseworthy in
themselves, must be placed against the backdrop of a society
in which sex was ignored, woman confined to a subservient position in the home, and institutionalized religion considered the

8. Prescott, "*Jane Eyre:* A Romantic Exemplum," pp. 97–98: "The
erotic strain which grows more and more pronounced as the narrative
unfolds differentiates the novel from other romances and exempla."

arbiter of all good Christian behavior. To complicate matters further is the fact that with half of her nature Charlotte Brontë was deeply conservative: she could admire Byron, but not sanction him. For every rebellious or natural instinct, therefore, her puritan conscience, her Victorian-inspired conservatism must have caused her agonies of guilt. The result, as I have tried to show, was a novel of rebellion written in the language of trial and punishment.

Publication confirmed that Miss Brontë had a great deal to be guilty about. While unofficial Victorians made the novel a best-seller, Mandarin Victorianism fell upon the book, condemning it as both repugnant and dangerous. Official Victorianism could respond to a missionary tract, could swallow Dickens's mild doses of prison reform, could contribute to the Jew's basket or to a fund for superannuated governesses; it could not sanction an ardent spirit which craved—not philanthropic aid, not legislation—but a dangerous and undefinable liberty. Riding to the attack, the influential *Quarterly Review* declared Jane Eyre to be insidiously dangerous, both for its "pre-eminently anti-Christian" stance and its "pervading tone of ungodly discontent" and rebellion: ". . . the most subtle evil which the law and the pulpit, which all civilized society in fact has at the present day to contend with . . . which has overthrown authority and violated every code human and divine abroad, and fostered Chartism and rebellion at home . . . ."[9]

Charlotte Brontë stubbornly denied that her novel was either irreligious, rebellious, or "coarse," but public criticism sank in deep. Having learned her lesson, she turned from private rebellion to social reform in her next novel, *Shirley*—and wrote her most impersonal, most self-conscious, most Victorian book.

9. Elizabeth Rigby [Lady Eastlake], "*Vanity Fair*—and *Jane Eyre*," *Quarterly Review* 84 (December 1848): 162–176.

CONCLUSION

The question of whether Charlotte Brontë's prose style is "good" or "bad" falls beyond the range or intent of this discussion. Too frequently value judgments about style tell us more about the bias of the critic and his age than about the style itself: the reaction against Shakespearean drama in the eighteenth century, for example, reveals a great deal about the tastes of that era, but relatively little about Shakespeare's art. The Romantic movement in British literature gave rise to the cult of individuality. Reflected in the prose of the first half of the nineteenth century, this cult promoted the relatively uninhibited expression of opinion, emotion, bias, and eccentricity: a strongly distinctive style was a good style. According to this standard Charlotte Brontë's idiosyncratic prose, like Carlyle's, is good, and Lucy Snowe speaks for Victorian taste in general when she says that she inevitably flagged over characterless books, preferring always those books "on whose style or sentiment the writer's individual nature was plainly stamped." And according to nineteenth-century rhetorical principles which considered poetry because of its economy and force the superior mode of expression, Brontë's style—insofar as it judiciously employs poetic device—is good.

Conversely, the twentieth century views both "poetic" prose and strong rhetoric with suspicion and distaste, agreeing with T. S. Eliot that more prose is bad because it is like bad poetry than poetry is bad because it is like bad prose, and rejecting heightened rhetoric for its inextricable association with the outmoded earnestness of the Victorians. There is little to argue, therefore, when W. A. Craik states that Charlotte Brontë's emphatic style is dated and antipathetic to present-day readers— even though that reaction may not be one's own. Rather than polemic defense, this investigation has therefore been concerned with a description of Brontë's prose style and the relationship of this formal medium to her fiction and personality.

From these explorations emerges the portrait of a style whose sum—because of the immiscible nature of its parts—is tension. Figurative and violent language exists side by side with the pedantic; the language as a whole is controlled by Brontë's use of short independent clauses and, more significantly, by antithetical balance, a trait that shapes both sentence structure and more complex formal elements such as plot structure, setting, and characterization. Inverted sentence structure creates a prose that is poetic on the one hand, perverse and jarring on the other. The emphatic adverb imparts sensibility to the prose, yet this sensibility is in sharp contrast to the didactic tone that Brontë's heavy use of the negative creates. On the lexical level, the language of trial and punishment in a particular novel, *Jane Eyre*, suggests a deep ambivalence in its author toward the very causes the novel champions. The totality is a prose vitalized by the unresolved battle of its conflicting parts. Indeed, as Leo Spitzer claims, "the lifeblood of the poetic creation is everywhere the same, whether we tap the organism at 'language' or 'ideas,' at 'plot' or at 'composition.'"

If, as this study asserts, style is in part *l'homme même*, then the "lifeblood" of Charlotte Brontë's personality must be an ambivalence resulting from the continual but unresolved conflict of opposing drives—a conflict which is the hallmark of the neurotic personality. While Charlotte Brontë has been labeled neurotic before, the ambivalence of her attitudes, her ideas—her life itself—have not adequately been stressed.

In London on a Sunday afternoon in December 1849 a group of ladies which includes Harriet Martineau waits in high expectation for the appearance in their drawing-room of Currer Bell, the unknown author of the best-seller, *Jane Eyre*.[1] Speculation runs rife. Will *he* be dashingly romantic like Rochester? Will *she* (Martineau suspects a woman) be eccentric or fiery as the sensationalism of the novel would seem to suggest? A ring at the bell; "Miss Brontë" is announced; and into the room walks a tiny figure hardly bigger than a child, clad in Quaker-like garments, with a plain, almost homely face and a manner that is winning, but much subdued and very shy: the creator of *Jane Eyre*. While this conflict between creator and creation is a superficial one, it is hardly irrelevant, for the contrast between Charlotte Brontë's unromantic appearance and her very romantic soul surely generated many of the conflicts that characterized her life.

There is, for example, Charlotte Brontë's attraction to both radical and conservative political thought, a paradox manifest in her two closest, life-long friendships: Ellen Nussey came from an old, high-Tory family, while Mary Taylor's family was notorious locally for its outspoken radicalism—and Charlotte Brontë was drawn to both casts of mind. Again, there is Brontë's craving for society to be matched against her equally strong craving for solitude. Most of her letters obsessively reiterate her despair at the loneliness, the isolation, the deadly sameness of the parsonage routine. Yet, when she did travel—to Ellen Nussey's, to London, to Miss Wooler's, to the Kay-Shuttleworth's—exhaustion and nervous irritation plagued her until she was driven back home. So many letters to Ellen Nussey concern visits proposed and visits postponed: one must conclude that this conflict lies at the root of both proposal and postponement. Or, consider her dutiful and lifelong preoccu-

---

1. Elizabeth Cleghorn Gaskell, *The Life of Charlotte Brontë* (London, 1960), p. 288. For a fuller account see R. B. Martin, "Charlotte Brontë and Harriet Martineau," *NCF* 7 (1952): 198–201.

pation with church duties as a parson's daughter against the surprisingly minor and negative part played by religion in her novels, an absence even more conspicuous considering the preoccupation of much Victorian literature with religious themes. Or, again, we can contrast her strong championship of individual worth against her priggish antipathy to her third suitor because he was not a "gentleman."

Another conflict exists in Charlotte Brontë's dutiful devotion to her father, even when that father inadvertently and advertently contrived to stifle her life, weighed against the fact that she makes nearly all of her protagonists—Crimsworth, Frances Henri, Jane, Rochester, Shirley, Robert and Louis Moore, Lucy Snowe—orphans. If a relative does exist, it is a female: Frances and Jane have aunts (who die) and Caroline Helstone finds her mother. When a father-figure exists, like Rochester or Paul Emanuel, he is either mutilated or drowned. Or there is her evident desire to be mastered by a superior person, expressed in both her novels and her letters, to be matched against heavy evidence from the same sources of a feministic resistance to such domination. Even her most timid, passive heroine, Frances Henri, rebels against the traditional feminine role. Sitting demurely on Crimsworth's knee just after she has consented to be his wife, she quickly introduces the subject closest to her heart —far closer, obviously, than her love for Crimsworth:

> "Monsieur est raisonnable, n'est-ce pas? . . . Well, Monsieur, I wished merely to say, that I should like, *of course,* to retain my employment of teaching. You will teach still, I suppose, Monsieur?"
> "Oh yes! It is all I have to depend on."
> "Bon!—I mean good. Thus we shall have both the same profession. I like that; *and my efforts to get on will be as unrestrained as yours—will they not,* Monsieur?"
> "You are laying plans to be independent of me," said I.
> "*Yes,* Monsieur . . . ." (*P*, p. 199)

This is highly subversive doctrine, the respectful "Monsieur" notwithstanding: not only does Frances insist upon working, but upon pursuing a career with "unrestrained" effort—not at

all the same thing. Equally subversive—and strikingly modern
—is Frances's discontent with the working woman's economic
inequality: " 'How rich you are, Monsieur! . . . Three thousand
francs . . . while I get only twelve hundred!' " (*P*, p. 200).[2]
The conflicting claims of feminine passivity and masculine
aggression in Brontë's personality are nowhere more tellingly
dramatized than in Lucy Snowe's ambivalent behavior in accepting a masculine role in the farce enacted for Madame
Beck's fête. While she consents to playing the part of a man,
she will not entirely relinquish her femininity by dressing appropriately for the part. She compromises: retaining "her woman's garb without the slightest retrenchments," Lucy adds vest,
collar, cravat, paletôt, hat, and gloves. Quite literally refusing
to wear the pants, symbolic of masculine sexual and social aggression, Lucy—and Brontë, as her career as a novelist writing
under a male pseudonym indicates—can still relish a masculine
role and perform it well, despite the liability of femininity. The
exhilaration Lucy feels on stage playing the role of the fop and
the revulsion she experiences afterwards is a pointed confirma-
tion of the neurotic ambivalence of Lucy and Brontë's mind.[3]
Modern psychology's axiom that one's greatest wish is simultaneously one's greatest fear surely formulated the conflicting
impulses that were so divisive in Charlotte Brontë's life.

With this understanding, hypotheses can be made with rea-
sonable certainty about other attitudes and opinions of the
author. We can speculate, for example, that the intense dislike,
even abhorrence, of women who are large, dark, and sensually
attractive expressed so frequently in the novels conceals an

2. Charlotte Brontë's comment upon reading Eckermann's *Conversa-
sations with Goëthe* that Eckermann's relationship to Goëthe was degrad-
ing is significant in that it contradicts the master-pupil ideal of the novels.
See letter to W. S. Williams, September 13, 1849, in Clement Shorter,
The Brontës: Life and Letters, vol. 2 (New York, 1908), pp. 70–71.

3. While it is not far-fetched to interpret the whole episode of Lucy's
performance as an instance of latent homosexuality, Karl Kroeber's comment that the transvestitism motif is attractive to Brontë because she
challenges the conventional roles assigned to men and women in her
society seems to me a sound explanation of the phenomenon (*Styles in
Fictional Structure* [Princeton, 1971], p. 92).

equally strong attraction toward just that type of woman. Or
we can guess that Charlotte Brontë's antipathy for the Catholic
Church is a reaction against a sensual and emotional appeal
that in reality had strong attractions for her, just as her sneers
at Catholics hide an unconscious envy of those who could give
themselves up to the comfort and security which she herself
admitted the Catholic religion could provide. Or we can hypothesize that a conflict between her ardent desire to be married and a rooted distaste for that same condition resulted in a
state of neurotic agitation that quite literally contributed to
her rapid decline after marriage, and to her death. "It was a
marvelous sight: a mighty revelation. It was a spectacle low,
horrible, immoral," cries Lucy Snowe upon viewing the acting
of Vashti (V, p. 220). One cannot help but feel that these almost simultaneous expressions of admiration and disgust char-
acterize very aptly the pattern of response controlling Charlotte
Brontë's life.

While many of these ambivalences seem purely personal, it
is not a simplification to find at the heart of them a basic conflict between a desire for freedom and the need to submit to
authority; or, in socio-economic terms, between the radical/
progressive and the conservative principle. Because this conflict
is essentially unresolved in Charlotte Brontë's mind, life, and
fiction, her position in the literary world of early and midnine-
teenth century England is rather exceptional. We have become
increasingly aware in recent years of a process that can be
traced with some regularity in the lives of many Romantic and
Victorian writers; a process that has come to be known as the
"Unlovely Compromise." That is, writers who begin in religious
doubt, political liberalism, poetry, and devotion to the imagination or the passions, end, often, in religious faith, conservatism,
prose, and reason: odes to nature and freedom are replaced
by odes to duty. In Wordsworth, Coleridge, Carlyle, Arnold,
Browning, Tennyson this—or a comparable metamorphosis—
can be traced. As this study reveals, Charlotte Brontë, on the
other hand, did not begin at one pole and end at the other: in
her life and in her fiction, similar opposing tendencies exist at
one and the same time, striving together in a battle from which

neither side emerges victorious. Speculations as to what might have been her development had she lived beyond her thirty-ninth year are interesting, but cannot alter the character of her life as we know it. A comparison of the parson's daughter with the profligate nobleman may seem rather ludicrous; yet perhaps only in Byron do we find so many conflicting personalities warring at once: Calvinist and libertine, radical and conservative, moralist and iconoclast. Byron's conflicts are fabulous, extreme, externalized: he lived them, trailing the pageant of his bleeding heart before the public eye. Charlotte Brontë lived quietly in a parsonage, suppressed one-half of her nature, fought its ambivalences. Perhaps it is because the cry of a Lucy Snowe is wrung forth from greater depths that it strikes us today as more tragic than a Childe Harold's.

Or a Heathcliff's. Despite the powerful fascination of Emily Brontë's hero, Heathcliff and his grand torments remain, I believe, outside the experience, and ultimately the sympathy, of most readers, who, like Lockwood and Nelly Dean, must regard with awe the brutal violence of Catherine and Heathcliff's passion. Unlike Charlotte Brontë's characters, Emily's protagonists are single-minded, living at a pitch of intense self-absorption that effectively removes them from any immediate connection with a social milieu. It is not surprising that from all biographical evidence, Emily emerges as a serene and monolithic personality, quite aloof from the social, moral, and personal conflicts against which Charlotte struggled all her life. This aloofness created an amazing novel, but it is Charlotte Brontë's novels which come to grips far more realistically with the problem of the human personality alienated from but necessarily involved in the world. Ultimately Lucy Snowe's struggle to forge a meaningful life for herself despite poverty, loneliness, mental anguish, and personal loss is a more significant subject than Catherine Linton's dying for love.

As creations of this divided personality, Charlotte Brontë's novels can be said to contribute something new to the canon of the British novel as it existed until her time. Let us, wrote E. M. Forster once in a different context, unite the poetry with the prose. In *Jane Eyre*, *Shirley*, and *Villette* the attempt has been made. Charlotte Brontë clearly indicates her reverence for the poet in *Shirley*, both in her description of the poet's existence in a pharisaical society, and later when Caroline calls the gift of poetry "the most divine bestowed on man" (*S*, pp. 36, 177); and her own poetic bias is closely woven into the texture of her prose. Sometimes the attempt is self-conscious, sometimes the result is crude; yet one should remember what Flaubert said about bad taste when he distinguished it from the simply ingenious: in order to have bad taste, one must have a sense for poetry, whereas ingenuity is incompatible with the genuinely poetic. Whatever its effect, the very presence of the poetic altered the form of the novel, and therefore its history.

For a telling example of this alteration, one has only to compare Fielding's use of poetic forms with Charlotte Brontë's. In Fielding's novels, figurative language and syntactic inversion, for example, do indeed occur—in the graveyard battle, in descriptions of Sophia, when Tom is discovered with Molly—but their effect is satiric, negative, and antipoetic. The mock-epic forms minimize, deflate, strip away. Look, Fielding is saying, how unepic, how unideal mankind can be: this is no epic battle but a skirmish over a whore. While he criticizes, however, Fielding at the same time confirms the social values of his age; poetic form in his novels functions conservatively as a corrective of institutions of which Fielding basically approves. Quite the opposite ends are achieved by poetic form in Brontë's fiction. Its function is rather radical in that it undermines social institutions by emphasizing man's alienation from society and his affinity to the extra-social: that is, to the life of the mind, the life of the imagination, to nature, to abstract ethical principle, to a god. In this sense can Brontë be said to have written romances rather than novels, for she is not first committed, like Fielding, Defoe, and Austen, for example, to the depiction of social convention—in Brontë's words, "the surface of life"—but to the problems of existing significantly outside it.[4]

4. Richard Chase argues that the Brontës domesticated myth; that although their novels contain the symbolism and myth typical of romance, the ending of *Jane Eyre* and *Wuthering Heights* represent "the triumph of the moderate, secular, naturalistic, liberal, sentimental point of view

In the sense that Charlotte Brontë's novels deal with protagonists who are essentially cut off from the rest of the world, they sound the note of alienation that was to become the central theme of late nineteenth- and twentieth-century fiction. Partly this alienation is forced upon the Brontë protagonist by his own obscure circumstances; partly this alienation is cultivated, for although her protagonists do not pretend to be artists, they claim a superiority which distinguishes them equally from the Philistine. One should not be misled by Brontë's proclaimed concern in the introduction to *The Professor* with the "homely and the plain" into thinking that these terms may be translated into the sentimental, the common, and the humble: her protagonists are not Victorian heroes in eclipse; she is not the singer of the everyday.[5] " 'Not three in three thousand raw school-girl governesses would have answered me as you have just done,' " Rochester tells Jane, but warns: " 'But I don't mean to flatter you: if you are cast in a different mould to the majority, it is no merit of yours: Nature did it' " (*JE*, p. 130). In all the novels, this "if" is resolved: Brontë heroes and heroines are indisputably "cast in a different mould."[6] They are removed from the common lot by virtue of their suffering, their ardent hearts, their ugliness, their incorruptible principles; their perversity; their solitude; their pride.

Of course, their principles are sometimes false, their judgments biased or silly, their hearts ardent for the wrong cause. George Eliot was right when she criticized *Jane Eyre* for its

---

over the mythical, religious, tragic point of view" ("The Brontës: A Centennial Observance," *Kenyon Review* 9 [Autumn 1947]: 487–506). Although Chase's point is well argued, the unresolved conflicts in Charlotte Brontë's nature, confirmed by her style, prevented, I believe, the "triumph" of either tendency. Whether mythic or not, the novels as a whole do not impress one as moderate, liberal, or sentimental.

5. Thus Mario Praz describes the characteristic Victorian protagonist in *The Hero in Eclipse in Victorian Fiction* (London, 1956).

6. Inga-Stina Ewbank, speaking of *The Professor*, calls Brontë heroes members of a "meritocracy" (*Their Proper Sphere* [London, 1966], p. 170). This apt term can apply, of course, to the whole collection of Brontë protagonists.

sacrifice to an ignoble and diabolical law.[7] At lowest ebb, the novels threaten to degenerate into the kind of bigoted insularity that inspired the Elizabethan plea, "From Turk and Pope defend us, Lord," for "Turkish tastes" and Catholicism occupy the author to a ridiculous degree. On the other hand, the energy with which these causes are advanced, and the ambivalences which the ardor exposes, vitalize the characters and the novels: neither degenerates into the mediocrity of compromise. José Ortega y Gasset has predicted that, because the nineteenth-century novel contains the least possible amount of poetic energy, it will be unreadable very soon "because the ideals attacked by it are hardly removed from the reality with which they are attacked. The tension is very weak: the ideal falls from a very small height."[8] Today *Jane Eyre* is as compelling as ever, and *Villette* is perhaps just beginning to win recognition as a masterly novel. If Charlotte Brontë's fiction does not become unreadable "very soon," it will undoubtedly be because in her novels the tension is not weak. As the tensions of her prose style indicate, life in her novels is not finally reduced to black and white because the ambivalences of the author's personality made her incapable of the kind of emotional rigidity that simplifies man's experience. Thus Charlotte Brontë's life and the fiction it produced can still speak to an era which recognizes the divided self as one of the central characteristics and concerns of modern man.

7. Letter to Charles Bray, June 1848, in *The George Eliot Letters,* ed. Gordon Haight, 7 vols. (New Haven, Conn., 1954–1955), 1: 268.

8. José Ortega y Gasset, *Meditations on Quixote* (New York, 1961), p. 163.

SELECTED BIBLIOGRAPHY

INDEX

SELECTED BIBLIOGRAPHY

Because this study of Charlotte Brontë's style necessarily adheres closely to the texts of her novels, the opportunity has not arisen to cite sources which must substantially influence any scholar of the Brontës as Victorian novelists: general works on the genre like Ian Watt's *The Rise of the Novel* (1957); studies about the Victorian period such as Walter Houghton's *The Victorian Frame of Mind* (1957) and Jerome Buckley's *The Victorian Temper* (1951); and, of course, many important general works on the Brontës themselves. The listings below tend to be formalistic in nature and are divided for convenience into two general categories: studies pertaining to Charlotte Brontë or the novel, and stylistic or linguistic studies that are particularly applicable to the analysis of literature.

CHARLOTTE BRONTE AND THE NOVEL

Brick, Allen R. "*Wuthering Heights:* Narrators, Audience, and Message." *CE* 21 (November 1959): 80–86.

Buckley, Vincent. "Passion and Control in *Wuthering Heights.*" *Southern Review* 1 (1964): 5–23.

Burkhart, Charles. "Another Key Word for *Jane Eyre.*" *NCF* 16 (September 1961): 177–179.

————. "Brontë's *Villette*." *Explicator* 21, no. 1, item 8 (September 1962).

Caudwell, Christopher. *Illusion and Reality*. New York: International Publishers, 1947.

Cecil, David. *Victorian Novelists*. Chicago: University of Chicago Press, 1958.

Chase, Richard. "The Brontës: A Centennial Observance." *Kenyon Review* 9 (Autumn 1947): 487–506.

Clark, William Ross. "The Hungry Mr. Dickens." In *Discussions of Charles Dickens*, edited by Clark. Boston: D. C. Heath, 1961.

Colby, Robert. *Fiction with a Purpose*. Bloomington: Indiana University Press, 1967.

————. "*Villette* and the Life of the Mind." *PMLA* 75 (1960): 410–419.

Coursen, Herbert R. "Storm and Calm in *Villette*." *Discourse* 5 (Winter 1961–1962): 318–333.

Craik, W. A. *The Brontë Novels*. London: Methuen, 1968.

Downing, Janay. "Fire and Ice Imagery in *Jane Eyre*." *Paunch* 26 (October 1966): 68–78.

Ericksen, Donald. "Imagery as Structure in *Jane Eyre*." *VN* 30 (Fall 1966): 18–22.

Ewbank, Inga-Stina. *Their Proper Sphere: A Study of the Brontë Sisters as Early Victorian Female Novelists*. London: Edward Arnold, 1966.

Flahiff, Frederick. "Formative Ideas in the Novels of Charlotte and Emily Brontë." *DA*, vol. 27, 746–747A (Toronto).

Ford, Boris. "*Wuthering Heights*." *Scrutiny* 7 (March 1939): 375–389.

Forster, E. M. *Aspects of the Novel*. New York: Harcourt, Brace, 1954.

Gaskell, Elizabeth Cleghorn. *The Life of Charlotte Brontë*. London: J. M. Dent, 1960.

Gérin, Winifred. *Charlotte Brontë: The Evolution of Genius*. Oxford: Oxford University Press, 1967.

Gregor, Ian, ed. *The Brontës*. Englewood Cliffs, N. J.: Prentice-Hall, 1970.

Hardy, Barbara. *The Appropriate Form: An Essay on the Novel*. London: Unversity of London, Athlone Press, 1964.

Heilman, Robert B. "Charlotte Brontë, Reason, and the Moon." *NCF* 14 (March 1960): 283–302.

————. "Charlotte Brontë's New Gothic." In *From Jane Austen to Joseph Conrad,* edited by Robert C. Rathburn and Martin Steinmann, Jr. Minneapolis: University of Minnesota Press, 1958.

Holgate, Ivy. "The Structure of *Shirley.*" *Brontë Society Transactions* 14 (1962): 27–35.

Johnson, E. D. H. "Daring the Dread Glance: Charlotte Brontë's Treatment of the Supernatural in *Villette.*" *NCF* 20 (March 1966): 325–336.

Kettle, Arnold. *An Introduction to the English Novel.* 2 vols. New York: Harper and Row, 1960.

Knies, Earl Allen. *The Art of Charlotte Brontë.* Athens, Ohio: Ohio University Press, 1969.

Korg, Jacob. "The Problem of Unity in *Shirley.*" *NCF* 12 (September 1957): 125–136.

Kroeber, Karl. *Styles in Fictional Structure: The Art of Jane Austen, Charlotte Brontë, and George Eliot.* Princeton: Princeton University Press, 1971.

Lodge, David. *The Language of Fiction.* London: Routledge and K. Paul, 1966.

Martin, Robert. *The Accents of Persuasion: Charlotte Brontë's Novels.* London: Faber and Faber, 1966.

————. "Charlotte Brontë and Harriet Martineau." *NCF* 7 (1952): 198–201.

Miller, J. Hillis. *The Form of Victorian Fiction.* Notre Dame: University of Notre Dame Press, 1968.

Millett, Kate. *Sexual Politics.* New York: Avon, 1971.

Ortega y Gasset, José. *Meditations on Quixote.* New York: Norton, 1961.

Praz, Mario. *The Hero in Eclipse in Victorian Fiction.* London: Oxford University Press, 1956.

Prescott, Joseph. "*Jane Eyre:* A Romantic Exemplum with a Difference." In *Twelve Original Essays on Great English Novels,* edited by Charles Shapiro. Detroit: Wayne State University Press, 1960.

Sanger, C. P. "The Structure of *Wuthering Heights.*" *Hogarth Essays.* No. 19. London: Hogarth Press, 1926.

Schorer, Mark. "Fiction and the 'Matrix of Analogy.'" *Kenyon Review* 11 (Autumn 1949): 544–550.

Shorter, Clement. *The Brontës, Life and Letters.* 2 vols. New York: Scribner's, 1908; repr. New York: Haskell House Publishers, 1969.

Solomon, Eric. "*Jane Eyre:* Fire and Water." *CE* 25 (December 1963): 215–217.

Tillotson, Kathleen. *Novels of the Eighteen-Forties.* Oxford: Clarendon Press, 1954.

Van Ghent, Dorothy. *Form and Function in the English Novel.* New York: Harper and Row, 1961.

Watson, Melvin. "Form and Substance in the Brontë Novels." In *From Jane Austen to Joseph Conrad,* edited by Robert C. Rathburn and Martin Steinmann, Jr. Minneapolis: University of Minnesota Press, 1958.

————. "Tempest in the Soul: The Theme and Structure of *Wuthering Heights.*" *NCF* 4 (September 1949): 87–100.

Wise, T. J., and Symington, J. A., eds. *The Brontës: Their Lives, Friendships, and Correspondence.* 4 vols. Oxford: Shakespeare Head Press, 1932.

STYLE AND STYLISTICS

Auerbach, Eric. *Mimesis: The Representation of Reality in Western Literature,* translated by Willard R. Trask. Princeton: Princeton University Press, 1968.

Bailey, Richard, and Burton, Dolores. *English Stylistics: A Bibliography.* Cambridge, Mass.: MIT Press, 1968.

Bowles, Edmund A., ed. *Computers in Humanistic Research: Readings and Perspectives.* Englewood Cliffs, N.J.: Prentice-Hall, 1967.

Carroll, John B. "Vectors of Prose Style." In *Style in Language,* edited by Thomas A. Sebeok. Cambridge, Mass.: MIT Press, 1960.

Chatman, Seymour, and Levin, Samuel, eds. *Essays on the Language of Literature.* Boston: Houghton Mifflin, 1967.

Craig, G. Armour. "On the Style of *Vanity Fair.*" In *Style in Prose Fiction,* edited by Harold C. Martin. New York: Columbia University Press, 1959.

Freeman, Donald C., ed. *Linguistics and Literary Style.* New York: Holt, Rinehart and Winston, 1970.

Gray, Bennison. "The Lesson of Leo Spitzer." *MLR* 61 (October 1966): 547–555.

Harris, Zelig. "Discourse Analysis." *Language* 28 (1952): 1–30.

Holland, Norman. "Prose and Minds: A Psychoanalytic Approach to Non-Fiction." In *The Art of Victorian Prose,* edited by George Levine and William Madden. London: Oxford University Press, 1968.

Jacobson, Roman. "Closing Statement: Linguistics and Poetics." In *Style in Language*, edited by Thomas A. Sebeok. Cambridge, Mass.: MIT Press, 1960.

_____. "The Metaphoric and Metonymic Poles." In *Fundamentals of Language*, edited by Jacobson and Morris Halle. 's-Gravenhage: Mouton, 1956.

Jespersen, Otto. *Growth and Structure of the English Language*. 9th ed. New York: Doubleday, 1938.

Kames, Lord Henry. *Elements of Criticism*. New York: A. S. Barnes, 1877.

Lee, Vernon [Violet Paget]. *The Handling of Words and Other Studies in Literary Psychology*. New York: Dodd, Mead, 1923; repr. Lincoln: University of Nebraska Press, 1968.

Lester, Mark, ed. *Readings in Applied Transformational Grammar*. New York: Holt, Rinehart and Winston, 1970.

Levin, Samuel. *Linguistic Structures in Poetry*. The Hague: Mouton, 1962.

Martin, Harold C. "The Development of Style in Nineteenth-Century American Fiction." In *Style in Prose Fiction*, edited by Martin. New York: Columbia University Press, 1959.

Merritt, Travis R. "Taste, Opinion, and Theory in the Rise of Victorian Prose Stylism." In *The Art of Victorian Prose*, edited by George Levine and William Madden. London: Oxford University Press, 1968.

Miles, Josephine. "Works on Style." In *Style and Proportion: The Language of Prose and Poetry*. Boston: Little, Brown, 1967.

Milic, Louis T. "The Computer Approach to Style." In *The Art of Victorian Prose*, edited by George Levine and William Madden. London: Oxford University Press, 1968.

_____. *Style and Stylistics: an analytical bibliography*. New York: Free Press, 1967.

Mukarovsky, Jan. "Standard Language and Poetic Language." In *A Prague School Reader on Esthetics, Literary Structure, and Style*, edited and translated by Paul L. Garvin. Washington, D.C.: Georgetown University Press, 1964.

Ohmann, Richard. "Generative Grammars and the Concept of Literary Style." *Word* 20 (December 1964): 423–439.

_____. "A Linguistic Appraisal of Victorian Style." In *The Art of Victorian Prose*, edited by George Levine and William Madden. London: Oxford University Press, 1968.

————. "Prolegomena to the Analysis of Prose Style." In *Style in Prose Fiction,* edited by Harold C. Martin. New York: Columbia University Press, 1959.

Osgood, Charles E. "Some Effects of Motivation on the Style of Encoding." In *Style in Language,* edited by Thomas A. Sebeok. Cambridge, Mass.: MIT Press, 1960.

Read, Herbert. *English Prose Style.* New York: G. Bell, 1928.

Riffaterre, Michael. "Criteria for Style Analysis." *Word* 15 (April 1959): 154–174.

Spencer, Herbert. *Philosophy of Style.* New York: D. Appleton, 1917.

Spencer, John, ed. *Linguistics and Style.* London: Oxford University Press, 1964.

Spitzer, Leo. *Linguistics and Literary History; Essays in Stylistics.* New York: Russell and Russell, 1962.

Uitti, Karl. *Linguistics and Literary Theory.* Englewood Cliffs, N. J.: Prentice-Hall, 1969.

Ullmann, Stephen. *Language and Style.* Oxford: B. Blackwell, 1964.

————. *Style in the French Novel.* Cambridge, Eng.: Cambridge University Press, 1957.

Wellek, René. "Leo Spitzer (1887–1960)." *Comparative Literature* 12 (Fall 1960): 310–334.

————, and Warren, Austin. *Theory of Literature.* New York: Harcourt, Brace and World, 1956.

Whately, Richard. *Elements of Rhetoric.* Edited by Douglas Ehninger. Carbondale, Ill.: Southern Illinois University Press, 1963.

INDEX

TEXT DESIGNED
BY IRVING PERKINS
JACKET DESIGNED BY KAREN FOGET
MANUFACTURED BY IMPRESSIONS, INC., MADISON, WISCONSIN
TEXT LINES ARE SET IN CALEDONIA, DISPLAY LINES IN
CENTURY NOVA AND CALEDONIA

Library of Congress Cataloging in Publication Data
Peters, Margot.
Charlotte Brontë.
Bibliography: p. 167–172.
1. Brontë, Charlotte, 1816–1855.   I. Title.
PR4169.P4   823 .8   72-7993
ISBN 0-299-06240-6